ACKNOWLEDGMENTS

I would like to thank John Jacobsen, who encourage me from the beginning of my writing. Who is and always will be an encouragement to me?

The brilliant book cover and design, would not have been possible, without the artistic creativity and talent of Trina Emigh

DISCLAIMER

In writing this book, I am not making any claim about the authenticity of any or all of these statements. Some have been fact-checked, and others have not. Some articles have been adopted from Facebook and or Tik Tok and the authors have been shown But I believe some are true, because of the times we live in, and the treatment of our fellowmen in the past and present day. Not all articles are totally the authors, because I made some altercations that would convey or fit my expression of the novel.

INTRODUCTION

Some may feel offended, by this book. But, how can I express myself, no one wants to hear the plight of African Americans without some negative feedback. This, society has used us 400 plus years, and to me, no one is trying the right the wrongs, America has imposed upon people of African descent. Every other nation or people, America has wronged, America has made restitution to them, except for people of African descent. Every, nationally that comes to this country, can get a foot up, except African Americans.

ECCLESIASTES 4:1-4 holds a special place in my heart; because it seems to speak directly to me.

1 So I returned and considered all the oppressions that are done under the sun: and behold the tears of such as were oppressed, and they had no comforter, and on the side of their oppressors there was power, but they had no comforter.

2 Wherefore, I praised the dead which are already dead more than the living which is yet alive.

3 Yea, better is he than both they, which hath not been, who hath not seen the evil work that is done under the sun.

4 Again, I considered all travail, and every right work, that for this a man is envied of his neighbor he is also vanity and vexation of spirit.

What will some men do, make him feel that he is better than another? The bible, tell us that money is the root of all evil. After 400 hundred years of slavery, when will the misery end? I ask myself, is there anyone in government, that will step up and say this is wrong. As I mention later in this book, how president Lyndon B. Johnson, said that the schools in the south, would integrate, not only did he say it, he made sure, his orders were carried out. Now, what we have today, is school integration in the south.

Slaves were the first, to be traded on the stock market. What I am getting at is when will liberty come to us. No one liked to have a conversation, about the atrocities or what was done by the Europeans to Africans. We, as Africans have given our hearts and souls, to this country. Then turn around and be hanged from a tree on the courthouse lawn. Which was, then. Now, they shoot us down in the streets. America has become so immune to the killing of Americans. A dog is treated better than that, Michael Vick, lost his football career, and when we complain, like Colin Kaepernick, or, show our feelings or actions, we're a troublemaker or labeled as a communist, this is why racism persists today. We; are human, just like the rest of America. We hurt, we cry, we have feelings, just like everyone else. The American system makes sure there is no unity or structure in the African family.

I have stopped watching television so much; it seems the only time the world like to see an African male is when he has a ball in his hand or runs with one. I notice commercials, they will put someone on television, that looks of African descent, but are not. After all these years of hard labor, we can't even get the land we worked for. The land is power, if you are trying to break a nation, what do you do? Keep them poor. How can someone?

live to their life potential, when you are bent on the destruction of your fellow man?

Some people, all their life has been a lie and they will do anything to keep the truth from coming out, because what will their children think of them to keep living that lie, cover-up history, and deny someone else their life, liberty, and pursuit of happiness. When the Europeans went to Africa, they not only stole slaves, they took a way of life, family structure, and unity, to make sure none of these values came to the new world with us, they turned us against each other, and right today, some of us, have those crabs in a barrel mentality.

I sometimes, sit and ponder the why. People say you can't get blood from a turnip. In the new world, people were, whatever their nationality was. Now this white and African is a man-made invention, the sad part about it is, the churches played a key role in racism, then you want to be numbered among Christ-like How can you say, you are a Christian; when you know the bible says, God, took one blood and created all nations and that he (God) has no respect of person, Now, here you come a "Christian" and have the respect for a person, the bible says, respect of person is a "sin" as too their financial or economic statics. There, is nowhere in the bible, that says Caucasians are the superior race. I, guess that's what's called, "a little white lie".

I hope some will read the printed articles and lead to some positive changes in how we as a people are treated.

CONTENTS

THE GREAT AND AWFUL LIE

Martin L. King and Muhammad Ali

Somebody told a lie one day, matter of fact, they told two lies. They couched it in a language that made everything black, ugly, and, evil. looking at the dictionary and seeing the synonyms of the word black, it's always something degrading, low, and sinister. They; played on words to the American public, for an instant, the little ugly duckling, was a black duck. The black cat; was bad luck. Just the word blackmail, and devils' food cake, then on the other hand miss America, was always white, the president, lived in the white house, then the killer, angel food cake, just to name a few. Look, at the word white, it was always, supposed to be something pure. I want to get the language right, I want to get it so, it can be said, yes, I am black and I'm proud of it.

MELANIN, WHAT'S THAT?

Mr. Imhotep facebook.com

Melanin is commonly associated with skin and that's what gives your skin its color, we call that pigment melanin. But it's also in your nervous system, which causes you to transmit information faster and store more information than in any other race. It's also in your bones which cause you to retain more minerals than any other race and of course, is in your muscle you have what we call fast-twitch reaction, have a faster reaction time and you have more vitamins and minerals in your muscles than any other race. melanin is also in your eyes that causes you to absorb more color than any other race and of course, is in your ears, that makes you absorb sound, so you will see colors differently than anybody else and you will hear differently so, therefore, your music will always be different and you always put together colors differently melanin is in your taste buds which cause you to have the ability to taste the full flavor of the food that you taste.

So, you always combine your food differently and when you eat somebody else food, that's why you will say that's bland. That's because; they don't have the flavors of food as you do. the melanin causes you to have this ability that's what we call the biochemical marker of life the more melanin you have the more civilized you are. The more melanin you have, the more psychic you are, you see what I'm saying the more melanin, the more human you are, that is what we're talking about we're talking about how to understand this unique ability to be human. To be melanated and how it would sustain you, the problem with this melanin, all drugs work by destroying melanin, it's not a drug unless it can destroy melanin. In some ways speed it up, slow down, or destroyed it. But they use different terms when they talk about melanin and they won't say melanin, they may say melatonin, which is made from melanin or they may say serotonin, these are hormones that are made from melanin.

You can read the literature says melatonin or serotonin reuptake inhibitor. which means it stops your body from using melanin, we simply use these big awkward terms, reuptake inhibitor. The problem is with science a very crude way to explain something that's the problem with science. you can arrive at the truth quicker with your spirituality; than you can with some science. I'll be clear on that, but don't get lost in this jargon, the science that I may use. just simply remember that you cannot have science without culture. culture perceives everything, you can't have biology without culture, you can't have a relationship without culture, and you don't know the words to use.

people are classified by their culture, men have short hair, women have long hair, women wear dresses, and men with pants that's what we call gender. So, gender helps you to even see the other sex, you can't relate to him without this gender stuff. man is supposed to do, women supposed to do that, that has nothing to do with nature that's just gender and gender you get from your culture. Your culture allows you to see each other and relate to each other. Culture is a combination of how you are chemical, so you would always have a different culture because the chemicals in your body are different, because of the melanin and we're back to the melanin again.

Melanin, tells how you grow, it tells your body it's time to be a teenager, you should have pubic hairs, just cycles in your life, but when you start messing with melanin a lot of stuff there, you're messing with the cycles of the person the rightists of their body messing with the digestive system, the reproductive system you messing with melanin that's the biochemical key to life that's how you measure the age of a mummy, how we measure the age of your brain how much melatonin. We don't use this word too much in science, probably because it would lead to black people, so we the world don't want to lead any information to black people because we want to establish that black people are dumb. let me start using the word melanin, then the question will arise, who has the most melanin now what are we talking about? Every time they have a melanin conference in the world which is every three years the Germans come, Italians come, the US comes, the Canadians come but no one black is ever invited or was ever intended to attend the melanin conference and that's done on purpose.

THE MOST SHOCKING SECRET ON THE PLANET

Jacqueline Battalora

The myth of the white race, which is not foundational law, and the matter of white supremacy. White people did not exist on planet earth until 1681. Any claim, that this group called white people, is rooted in biology derived from genes or nature is a LIE. As, a matter of foundational law, white supremacy has been embedded in the United States of America from its founding as a matter of law.

Now, I don't expect you to get all that, at least not now. But we have to begin this conversation in colonial North America, specifically the British Colonies of Maryland and Virginia. Both were British Colonies and both shared particular characteristics, their economies were rooted in tobacco farming. If you know anything about tobacco farming, it requires tremendous human labor. So, those who own large plantations and big landholders, constantly needed laborers to do the work and grow tobacco, in addition to sharing an economic base, both Colonies had an incredible gender imbalance of roughly 10 men for every woman.

Now, who constituted the people in these two colonies? This was the early 1600s, the early part of the 17th century, in colonial North America. England, for some bizarre reason, until this day, cannot be explained, there was a population boom in England in the early 17th century. So, there were lots of poor British people, who were on the public doles that couldn't find a way to make a living, who could not feed themselves. So, the king of England; was quite happy to have them sign a contract of indentured service, to then go work in the British colonies.

So, that is what happened, both indentured and enslaved persons according to history were bought, sold, and traded like cattle, but of course, not all laborers stand equal in terms of their labor agreements or lack thereof. Those who came under a term of indenture worked for a term of years and presumably, this indenture was an agreement that they chose to enter into, the terms of indenture were largely protected by British law. Although the terms that took form in colonial North America, were quite different than those that existed in England, for example, indentured servants could marry because that was viewed as the way to produce the next group of workers in that country, and indenture servants were prohibited from marrying and if a woman were unfortunate enough to get pregnant during their terms of indenture, they added usually about 7 to 9 years onto their term of indentured and one year to the father.

Slavery, of course, was a status that came with life, work for life, there was neither British law nor international law to prohibit or restrict slavery, at this period in colonial North America, there were free persons of African descent, we know that landholders freed slaves. They did so in Wills, they did so, by allowing them to purchase their freedom or the freedom of a family member.

The vast majority of workers in colonial North America at this time were British men. There were some women, there were some European laborers from Portuguese,

Dutch, Ireland, and Scotland. There were small numbers of persons of African descent and even smaller numbers of members of native tribes.

Again, there were British, Europeans, Africans, and members of native tribes. Here's what I find folks have the most difficult time with. We struggle with getting a good picture of social life, the social context at this juncture was very good; and understanding of the social relations that existed. But pre-Bacons rebellions society is something that we generally in this country struggle to grasp, so I'm going to do my best to paint a picture of the period

What we know, is that British and African laborers worked, ate, and slept together, furthermore the evidence from this period, which covers the first ¾ of the 17th century, the anecdotal evidence reveals that they lived under similar conditions and faced the same opportunities, with chances to make it once one was free of their term of service, which was enslavement or indentured. British laborers constituted the vast majority of the population in both colonial Maryland and colonial Virginia.

The law of coverture; is derived from British common law and it structures marriages, the man and woman become one and the one is the man. The woman didn't have the right to retain her- wages, she couldn't create a state planning, wills, or search without the approval of a man. So, all men who were free of indenture or enslavement, face the same opportunities in these Colonies as a matter of law for example a free man of African descent could own servants or slaves and they did, they could vote and they did, and they could marry persons of the opposite gender regardless of national origin marriages between men of African descent and women primarily of British descent were not uncommon, in one county, ½ free man of African descent was married to a European woman, there was a challenge to these marriages, but it did not come from the masses, but the elites.

Colonial Maryland lawmakers passed a law in 1664, punishing British and other freeborn women, who married enslaved Negro men. The punishment for entering into these marriages; was that the woman, herself would be enslaved for her husband's natural life, and any children, they had, would be enslaved into their 20s. Now, these marriages were encouraged by property owners, because in fact, such a marriage increases their property value. This law of 1664 represents, if not the first, certainly the precursor to the anti-miscegenation law.

These are laws, that punish prohibited marriages, notice that white people didn't exist yet until 1664, at least as referenced in that law. But most generally speaking and anti-miscegenation law prohibited and punish marriages between a white person and a specific nonwhite person or persons. But let me be really clear, the only marriages that anti-miscegenation laws prohibited with those between a white person and always a person of African descent and sometimes various other groups.

Anti-miscegenation laws shape the faces of these groups of these so-called, white people. So, they pass the law of 1681 and this law made it illegal for British and other white women to from marrying a negro slave furthermore the law punishes any landholder who encouraged the marriages and any religious authority who performed it.

This law equals the invention of the human category called white people. Did this group of laborers, some of whom are from Portugal, Holland, Ireland and Scotland did today a little genetic transformation that occurred right after the general assembly in Maryland meet creating a genetic sludge that we can now call white? Virginia passed its first anti-miscegenation law in 1691, Virginia, the law prohibited both white men and white women from marrying a person of African descent or a member of a native tribe, but I leave you thinking that gender equality was being created in this law, let me quickly dispelled that.

Studies of antebellum courts; revealed that; anti-miscegenation law, was in a language prohibiting these marriages for white men and women, so we know from antebellum court cases that plenty of white men, married and were engaged in intimate sexual relations with prohibited women, however, very rarely where they brought to court and punished under the anti-miscegenation law, very rarely. Now, let's look at the relationship between Thomas Jefferson the third president, like it was said earlier, the white male was very rarely punished, but that is a white supremacist from our founding father and Sally Hemings was a child.

So, here pay attention to this law in its enforcement is largely focused on controlling the relationality and the sexuality of white women and nonwhite men, furthermore think about the enforcement practices that come out of this particular law, and what was the result who becomes more available for who? we see a further step in locating patriarchal power squarely among and within white men.

we talked about the law of 1664 and the amendments to that law, and the law of 1681 and we noted that the key difference between those two is the reference to the group was of concern, the language has shifted from British and other freeborn, to British and other white women on in a particular law so the question becomes well, what had happened between 1664 and 1681 and the answer is Bacon's rebellions.

There, was a massive revolt, in the colony of Virginia, that lasted more than a year. Let's talk about some background, of the seeds of this rebellion. what helps give rise to this violent outburst. Those who were enslaved on the topic, it's hard to imagine, were by definition of their status disgruntled laborers, and remember, that pool of readily available workers from England, who were poor and sent off into the guts of ships, well, that dried up.

There was no longer a pool of laborers from Britain, available to handle the work on the plantations in the Colonies, the results are they began to impose harsher punishments on indentured servants who were already there. So, that relatively minor infractions would result in significant extensions to their years of service, those who completed their term of indenture or who were released from their status as enslaved were frustrated because the king of England gave almost all of the farmable land to his buddies, even if they could find land to grow tobacco on, prices dropped and taxes went up. So, land and other opportunities became much more limited.

Nathanial Beacon; did not have to search very far for disgruntled laborers, those who were enslaved or indentured faced worse treatment, and those freed faced less ability to make a future for themselves. Persons of

European and African descent fought in the first phase of Bacon's rebellion against members of native tribes and then in the second phase of Bacon's rebellion against the British ruling elite.

Nathanial Bacon ultimately died from wounds he received in battle and England send troops into the colony, eventually, they squash the rebellion, but not without having made a significant impression, upon those who willed authority and were threatened by this rebellion, remember this rebellion lasted over a year and records from lawmakers in Virginia to the legal oversight authority in England revealed that over 30% of the population were in support of the rebellion.

Here, were the lessons from Bacon's rebellion a united labor force is a threat to the form of capitalism taking hold in the Colonies. Virginia lawmakers wrote letters to the oversight authority in London explaining that they intended to pursue a divide and conquer strategy to prevent future rebellion. It's only after Beacon's rebellion, that we see the emergence of white people as a group of humanity.

1681 some lawmakers invent a new label for a group of people, imagine if you will just for a second, for fun, that I'm a lawmaker and I just pass a law claiming that 75 out of a 100 are crunches, ¾ of you crunches and the other quarter of you are not, who would care? some silly lawmaker came up with a label for you it's really unlikely that would mean much, but let's say I follow with this, those who are crunches, you can pay no more than $25.00 a night for a hotel room, the crunches are first to come into any room at this conference and the first to leave, the first in line at the bathroom at any lunch counter and any other line that forms and the first to get to leave and that these privileges and advantages that come by this label, I must be special, imagine you're not crunchy, you might think, what's wrong with me this is not fair.

Laborers, before Bacon's rebellion, live the same lives they face the same opportunities rights, and privileges once they were free from enslavement or free from indenture that' was about to change. A slew of laws was passed in the decades after Bacon's rebellion and continued to get passed into the first quarter of the next century.

The first slew of laws included the prohibition of free blacks from holding public office prohibition of blacks and native tribal members from marrying whites; and the requirement that whites upon completion of their terms of service be paid goods, including guns and gunpowder a prohibition of free blacks from possessing a weapon, which meant that he could not protect himself or his family. Prohibition of blacks testifying against whites, these laws began to give a different meaning to these labels that before this moment just referenced where your nation men were in controlled off and land, the man had the control but the exchange was that in exchange for that authority he protects, that's the tradeoff for parochial power. of origin was, no anymore woman or their spouse, their children, and they have the legal authority to do so including severe beatings. control on all financial assets want to return quickly to a law that prohibited free blacks from possessing a weapon, what this law did was essentially stripped free black men of their ability to hold patriarch power, look under the law of coverture here's how things worked,

Now, this new law strips free black men, which made it impossible on by this law, and then, this law prohibited blacks from testifying against whites, we will see that threw out U.S. history, Mexicans were prohibited from testing against whites, Chinese prohibited from testifying against whites, and then it just becomes mongrels. The label went on to include persons of Japanese descent and the likes, so that's a law we see throughout U.S. history.

when you look at these laws, what's the message to white people each one of these laws? a message to this new group of people called white folks, on the one has and a message to those who it denies or restricts on the other. This package of laws, first passed after Beacon's rebellion did something extraordinary. Let's say that a single light in your home, represents the land-holding elite the 1%, and this represents the socioeconomic ladder in the colony, so this left hand over here represents this new group of laborers called white, and the right hand over here represents labors of African descent and members of native tribes, before Bacon's rebellion, these laborers lead the same lives, face the same opportunities and that changed.

But, when you look at these laws that pass, that created this change, it divided and created different meanings from this group vs. that group, but it didn't do a whole lot to lift the economic status of white people closer to that of the white elites, very little movement up.

What it did do was, it plummeted the bottom, created a new bottom to colonial society and shoved persons of African descent, and made members of native tribes there, so let's look at this group of humanity called white people. We, learn from this history, that white people were built upon the idea that the British had of themselves as white as Christian as freeborn as deserving of rights and privileges from which others can be denied. Until this day, white people have not been defined as a matter of law.

History teaches us that white, is the tool by which the laborers were divided those who shared the same living conditions, the same opportunities now experience ourselves is more connected with Paris Hilton than with our African American neighbor even though our economic status is far more similar to that neighbor, then to the lives of the 1%, but not only did this new organization of society created a new bottom, it created a link that heretofore had not existed, that connected this new group of laborers called white people with the elite and what was that connection this shared status called white imbedded with the presumption of its superiority the other thing to note about the invention of white people and the meaning of white of this history reveals is that white constituted the center of patriarchal power and we see that most clearly through anti-miscegenation law specifically for its enforcement.

We move from the 17th century into the 18th century, the American revolution has taken place and the first Congress of the United States of America will meet for the first time, and when they meet, they will establish laws regarding citizenship in this new country. the building is actually in New York where the first Congress meet here or the man who represented the first congress. These laws regarding citizenship include an area of law called naturalization law, naturalization law provides the process by which one who was not born in this country can become a citizen.

The first Congress of the United States determined in 1790 that to become a naturalized citizen of this new Republic called the United States of America, one had to be white, this was valid law in the United States until 1952, you had to be white to be a U.S. citizen. 1952 now as often, the case law impacts those who are gendered female differently than that gendered male with the naturalization law, for example, white women who were citizens if they dare to marry a man who was ineligible for citizenship via the naturalization law in other words, he was not white she loses her citizenship these laws worked to make white women most available to white men and frankly all women are available to white men.

The requirement of whiteness and naturalization law has had a significant impact on various groups of people who have come to the United States of America the naturalization law was a significant piece of evidence used in the Plessey vs. Ferguson case in 1896 to determine that U.S. citizenship status and therefore the protections of the constitutions were never intended to be applied to persons of African descent, naturalization law assured that the masses of Chinese laborers and Japanese laborers and then various other groups of laborers who came to this country would remain cheap dependents labor.

Why? because even though they were significant in numbers especially relative to their employer, or landholders in railroad companies if you're not white you're not a U.S. citizen if you're not a U.S. citizen; if you can't vote you can't place your political needs and desires thereby reducing these groups of people too dependent cheap labor in addition naturalization law was used to block persons of Chinese and Japanese and Filipino.

So, we could go on and on about various groups not only did this result in them getting paid less for doing the same job, all kinds of taxes got imposed on them, foreign wage tax various laws were passed to block them from being able to work in the public sector, block them from being able to hold a managerial position and then, of course, alien land laws were passed these were laws that made it illegal for those ineligible for naturalization of the not white people to own property and so what was the result of these laws for white people.

We; are really good about seeing the harm that these laws caused for certain groups, but let's get to the flip side of that point. When; I make land ineligible to purchase for certain groups, it makes more land available and cheaper for white people. when you're the lowest paid worker and prohibited from moving up as a matter of law. Those positions, they get paid more for are desirable or more available to white people.

WHY WERE MOST SLAVES, IN THE NEW WORLD, AFRICANS AND WHY DID EUROPEANS ENSLAVE AFRICANS?

PBS Origins facebook.com

Why, were most slaves in the new world, Africans, especially considering West Africa was thousands of miles away, from the Americas and Europe? Slavery has existed in multiple forms, throughout history and across a wide variety of cultures, but slavery in early America, meaning the North American Colonies, Central America and South America, and the Caribbean was ultimately powered by the labor of enslaved Africans and their decedents and there's an important question that people don't stop to ask, why Africans? there was nothing inherent to the social or psychological make-up of West Africans and their descendants in the 17th through 19th centuries that made them more prone to enslavement.

So, to get to the heart of the question we should first ask ourselves why did the Europeans set out to colonize the Americas, to begin with? So, before I dive into the answers to these questions, I think it's important to note that there is no such thing as benevolent slavery sense any system that is predicated on exploitation and extraction of labor through violence and force cannot be considered as fair, however, the purpose of this rough timeline is to sketch a comparison without creating higher archivable values of assessing harm inflicted on enslaved people to set the scene of the early American colonies.

European powers such as Spain followed by Portugal, Dutch, British, and French ventured out in search of conquest and capital their early expirations of the Americas starting in 1492 and continuing up unto the 18th century now weren't driven by wanderlust and desire for adventure no matter what Disney-filed versions we learned in Pocahontas. Instead, they were looking for one primary thing: wealth and this could mean gold and silver or it could mean land, farmland, and commercial crops.

The driving incentive for exploration was to increase European Power and fatten the royal coffers. But initially, slavery was not the source of this wealth. The early Spanish colonists to Central and South America in the 16th century rested in control of silver and gold mines that had been controlled by the Incan and Aztec empires. By forcing native groups to extract silver and gold from the mines they had already established, colonists were able to meet their desires for high profits with low labor costs, they had no intentions of paying anyone and the colonist was brutal.

By working native people to death, cutting off limbs, if they didn't extract enough materials quickly, or threatening them with murder, the Spanish were able to increase their mining effects in these regions and meet their specific demand for increased wealth through the 16th century. And despite European expectations, in other regions like North America or the Caribbean, there weren't huge repositories of gold and silver to send back to Europe.

But even though there was little precious metal to be found, the monarchies and the early colonists who arrived in these areas were equally intent on yielding high profits. So, they turned to crops that yielded high profits, like sugar, tobacco, rice, and then later cotton. To assure the highest profits, they began to look to slavery, since European laborers and indentured servants required payments or other forms of protection. So, next, we have to ask, when did colonists in the Americas turn to the African continent as a site for extracting slaves?

The first enslaved Africans arrived in the North American colonies under the control of the British in 1619, when 20 were forcibly transported to Jamestown, Virginia by the Dutch. But the first enslaved Africans had arrived in the Caribbean and Latin America before that, starting as early as the first decade of the 16th century. Because remember folks: the colonies were established in the Americas South, North, and Central America plus the Caribbean and not just the present-day US.

But the transportation of African people into slavery began before the colonization of the Americas. According to an article by Professor Hakim Adi, the Portuguese began enslaving Africans in the 15th century, when they arrived on the African continent for trade. Around that time there were enslaved Africans in Portugal. So, even though it was not the only or necessarily most widespread form of slavery at the time, this 15th-century precedent would set the stage for later decisions surrounding slavery that were to come in during colorization in the Americas.

But then, captivity was not extended exclusively to black people or people from the African continent and was often the result of raids, warfare, or slave trading that included Islamic traders, West African groups, and Europeans among others. Ok, we have established the precedents leading up to the explosion of the West African slave trade.

So, our final question is: Why did European colonists start to look exclusively at West Africans as the source of the slave trade? How did the emergence of chattel slavery in the Americas make it different from pre-existing forms of slavery? Remember that the colonies were established to make money for royal families, wealthy colonists, and the small class of wealthy colonists who owned large plantations and who looked to increase their margins by through not paying for the labor that generated their cash crops. So, it was not that slavery was needed to develop the colonies, but rather that it was decided that this was the quickest way to enrich people invested in getting rich.

Black slaves continued to arrive in the Caribbean, North America, and South America throughout the 16th, 17th, and 18th centuries, and it was not until the 19th century that slavery began to be eradicated, however by this point there was a large slave population in the Americas and the condition of slavery was considered legally hereditary, with children taking the status of their mothers in perpetuity.

When Europeans arrived in the Americas, colonists found that the previously established system that relied on enslaving conquered enemies was not functioning for several reasons, namely: Attempts to enslave native Americans prove difficult cause they had familiarity with the terrain of their nations and land. As a result, the potential for escape or revolt was high. This made using a system of leading raids and then enslaving whoever lost the battle less achievable; since colonists had little to no idea how to survive in these new regions and often fell prey to diseases to which the Europeans had no immunity.

The subsequent rampant genocide of native American people and the introduction of new diseases that decimated their population smallpox from Europe made widespread enslavement less possible. But by transporting people from west Africa to the Americas, European colonists wanted greater ability to control enslaved populations by making escape more challenging and reducing the risk of those who did flee blending into neighboring native nations.

Although the fact that there continued to be slave revolts amongst enslaved Africans and their descendants from 1-Africa proves that this calculation was often mistaken. 2-West Africa was often the source of forced and kidnapped laborers because of its proximity to sea ports. Which made contact between these three locations more possible. Also, laborers from West African countries were more familiar with the agricultural methods needed for mass cultivation of these kinds of crops in the new world. Well even though the slave trade brought an estimated 12 million people here as cargo, colonists eventually resorted to reproduction within the colonies as a method for sustaining slavery.

This meant that slavery could be passed down as an inherited status from mother to child. And to justify this never-ending enslavement we started to see the evolution of the false race, science racialization used as a justification for why one group of people, people of African descent were the only ones who could be enslaved.

But the shift erased the reality that before turning to West Africa as a labor source, slavery existed across racial lines, and was dictated more by battles and military capture than by skin tones. The resulting ideas we had about race evolved out of a desire by people engaging in the slave trade to find an after-the-fact justification for enslaving people from one specific region over others.

IT'S TIME, TO PULL THE LIE DOWN!

Minister Clarence McClendon

Because our founding fathers and the framers of the Declaration of Independence and the constitution of the United States; were predominantly men of faith and indeed this nation. The United States of America was founded upon religious freedom, their governing principles and governing premises their governing conclusion and constructs have been accepted as acceptable.

Yet, when it comes to the moral, ethical, and equal treatment of the men and women they brought to this nation from the African continent and enslaved them, canonized and codified into law and immoral unethical, and unacceptable lies, reducing black men and black women to property and the 3/5 of a human being, thus creating another race of people to be bought and sold and owned.

So, the same men who penned the words of the Declaration of Independence, we hold these truths to be self-evident that all men are created equal, that they are endowed by their creator with certain inalienable rights, and among these are life liberty and the pursuit of happiness, the same men who wrote that also codified and canonized in their constitution that the men and women that they brought over from Africa and enslaved were 3/5 of a human being.

In the law, they said that five slaves equal 3 three people. This is codified into law, look and get in the drawings of the constitutional amendments of 1787 and you will find this 3/5 law, that slaves were 3/5 of a human being, then with a good Christian conscience enslave another man or woman unless you first reduce them to being something less than human something less than, then you created another race and you can with a good Christian conscience go to bed owning other men and women. so, you created another race, which will make you comfortable in your western European imperialistic Christianity.

The 3/5 compromise of 1787 is what happened here this was because they were trying to decide, how the states at this time, the 13 colonies or states would be taxed and they were trying to figure out how they would get representation for presidential elections. The Southern states; had so many more people, they had slaves the northern states didn't want the southern states because they were slaveholders to have a larger population and therefore get larger representation in Congress.

More votes to vote for president so the creation of race was economic, it was about property and power, not about people and so they think it's compromised with slavers both personal population for the census count, 5 slaves equal three people and so another race was created.

Now, I declare to you that one of the reasons, that the Christian Church in the West has lost its power and its influence has lost its integrity with a generation of people, who neither know your God nor care about your forefathers is because of this life has been perpetually perpetuated in pulpits by white preachers and black preachers alike and it's time to pull the lie down.

TRANSATLANTIC SLAVE TRADE

The Infographic facebook.com

Transatlantic slave trade, 210 million Africans were taken from their homeland, shipped across the ocean, and forced to work under brutal conditions in the Americas. The trip itself, known as the middle passage was a horrible death, and inhumane experience the conditions on slave ships were dirty, scary, and offered no amount of comfort to the enslaved passengers.

There, were over 12,000 slave ships, making over 40,000 trips over 250 years of the slave trade; Just to name a few, Jesus of Lubeck, The Clotilda, HMS Black Joke, Antelope, Isabella, HMS Monkey, Segunda Rosario, Donna Marianna, Henrietta Marie and last but not least, The Amistad. Like, As I mentioned earlier 20 million Africans were transported by slave ships.

A British slave ship, the Zong 1781 massacred 132 sick and dying slaves, which were thrown overboard, in an attempt to collect insurance on their cargo

So, we're going to take a look at the brutal, misery of life on the slave ships, slavery was part of African society long before the arrival of European slave traders. But, the type of slavery practiced in the African tradition, was very different, captives who could be debtors, prisoners of war, or political prisoners were traded within the continent as a sign of wealth.

But slaves were not considered chattel with the influx of Islamic merchants, slaves from Africa were transported to the Mediterranean and later to the Americas by European merchants, when Europeans arrived in Africa, they first tried to raid the area themselves those raids weren't particularly successful. So, Europeans changed strategies and began buying enslaved people from African slave traders in places like the Kingdom of the Congo, the influx of European money proved highly tempting, and African traders started raiding nearby areas to acquire more people to sell to the Europeans.

Captives from throughout Africa were brought together in port cities to be transported across the Atlantic Ocean as they moved around from place to place on their journey towards the coast, enslaved Africans would be chained to one another. In the slave trade, the people in these ships; came from completely different backgrounds, and spoke different languages, they may never have even seen the ocean before. Another certain thing had never been on a ship like the ones they were about to board once at the port city.

Slaves were marched onto ships and put below deck after being freed former slaveholder Do Equiano, who was active in the abolition movement in England in the 18th century, wrote about his experiences when it came to his journey on a slave ship, as we all know he wasn't sure if the white men were going to kill him or eat him, once he was on board, he saw in his own words a multitude of black people of every description chained together.

Every one of their countenances expressed dejection and sorrow he was so terrified he fainted, the chains used on the enslaved Africans would chafe and dig into their skin, making movement painful many of the captives would quickly find themselves tethered to the dead. slave ships were designed to carry hundreds of people but in the interest of profit, they were usually severely overcrowded.

Captives were often packed into the ship so, tightly that they had no more than a few feet to move sit or sleep. Conditions were so cramped that the enslaved, wouldn't even have been able to find a bucket to defecate or urinate in, thus forcing them to stand things depicting the conditions on the infamous ship. The Brooks, which were later, a key exhibit in the argument against the slave trade, showed how slaves were to be put below deck. carried on the slave ships before the passage of the regulation act of 1788 100 slaves, after the law was passed, regulations restricted the number of captives aboard to about 450 in his memoirs.

Equiano also described what met him, when he went below deck on the slave ship according to the man himself, the first thing he was hit by, was an ungodly stench like he had never experienced in his life, it was so overpowering he was unable to eat and he wished death to relieve him. it is known that slaves were sometimes taken above deck and bathed if weather permitting, but it didn't make much of a difference, periodic washings were no match for the brutal conditions, and the punishment for captives who didn't listen to the crew tried to escape or showed any sign of defiance.

When; he refused to eat, one held him by the hands and feet, while the other flogged him severely, according to another source, if slaves refused to participate in the daily exercise deemed necessary for the preservation of their health or if they went about, it reluctantly or did not move with agility A cat with nine tails would often be used to administer the punishment.

branding and torture devices, were also frequently employed to drive enslaved into submission, when insurrections did break out from time to time those participating would be met with fierce punishment. Many captives felt they had nothing to lose, some slaves would rise against the crew regardless of the risks, and they typically found themselves facing cannon fire muskets and more bloodshed. Captives were only allowed to go topside when the weather permitted otherwise, they stayed in the heat and stench below deck with hundreds of people bound together in such a small space.

Equiano said things became pestilential, conditions bread disease among the captives according to his writings the crowdedness the climate was altercating, the conditions made everyone sweat, profusely and the air soon became unfit for respiration from a variety of loathsome smells, many of the slaves became sick and died, the inhumane conditions on slave ships encouraged the spread of disease particularly dysentery also known at the time as the flux, in his accounts from his time at sea, slave merchant John Newton describes numerous captives dying due to the flux and the fear of outbreaks sweeping over the ship according to one former ship's surgeon.

The floor of the rooms; was so covered with the blood and mucus, which had preceded them and consequence of the flux, that it resembled a slaughterhouse. Other diseases measles malaria and smallpox were also common and the mortality rate on slave ships was as high as 15% given the chance many of the enslaved tried to end their own lives their methods however would vary according to John Newton, captives might refuse to eat but try to poison themselves, others would try to jump overboard into the sea, to prevent this, many ships were outfitted with suicide Nets.

Even if someone could get through the Nets, many ships would send boats out to bring them back and it wasn't for altruistic reasons to the crew any enslaved person lost along the way, mental reduction of profits because they were deemed better for labor. The majority of captives were men but women were enslaved too, on the ships men and women were kept apart from one another, women and girls were often not, and, on some slave, ships the captain slept in a hammock, over the girls but.

The women faced some dangers that were different from what the men faced namely, they could be sexually brutalized by the crew, John Newton recorded a story about one of his crewmen assaulting a pregnant woman, aboard his ship according to Newton a man named William Cooney seduced a woman slave down into the room and lay with her. Given the whole quarter deck as punishment for the offense which Newton believed was the first of its kind on his ship, he had Cooney placed in irons and swore if anything happens to the woman, I shall be imputed to him or she was big with a child for reasons of profitability keeping their human cargo alive throughout the trip was essential to the crew members they did whatever it took to get them to eat.

The slave's diet included bread, beans, and salted meat. They were flogged as much to punish them as to demonstrate to the other captives that resistance was not tolerated take the story of a slave who was transported on the loyal George the ship that crossed the Atlantic to Barbados in 1727, he refused to

eat until he was reduced to mostly skin and bones and became sick the captain of the ship Timothy Tucker became outraged and began to fear that the slaves' actions might inspire the other 200 captives he had on board.

So, he had his cabin boy fetch a large horsewhip to flog the slave with but in this case, it didn't work despite the captain threatening to kill the slave the man simply replied "aroma" which in his language essentially meant so be it, on slaves, they used a special piece of equipment, called the speculum oris, which was a long thin mechanical contraption, used to force open unwilling throats to receive gruel and hence sustenance.

After at least six to eight weeks aboard the ship, enslaved people arrived at a port in the Americas and they didn't know what would happen next according to Equiano, at first the slaves believed that they were going to be eaten, but the slavers brought some older slaves from land to pacify them slaves and they were not to be eaten. where they would see many from their own countries Equiano much after we were landed. We saw Africans of all languages, and after that, they were immediately taken to a merchant's yard, where they were pent up together like so many sheep in a pool without regard to sex or age at this point the trip was over but the nightmare of enslavement had just begun.

WHEN THE ATROCITIES BEGAN

Henry Louis Gates

For those, who survive the middle passage. they don't want to talk about, how you got robbed of your name your Language, religion, your God, and your history, that's a subject they don't want to deal with and that's why they marked our time of arrival to 1619, have you ever wondered why they had a program on television called the $64 question, then the $64,000 question why 64, why not 63, why not 65.

The first slaves; came to North America on a ship named Jesus' captained by an English slave trader named Sir John Hawkins, some called him Sir John Hopkins in the year 1555, and from 1555 to 1619 is 64 years of the hidden history of how they broke a proud black man and turned him into a slave. what happened? they mated us. You heard, Tavis Smiley the other night, asked me playing the devil's advocate, so what about all these unwed mothers in all these drugs and all this stuff that black people are doing? and I said yes brother but that's a condition, that's an effect, what's the cause?

There was the breaking of the slave, there was the breeding of the slave, selling and merchandising of the slave, we were broken, because they took the babies from the mother, that's why you don't know your mother tongue, and Mama, prayed in a loud voice so you could pick up the name of your mother tongue. Most of the slaves, that was brought out of Africa were Muslims from West Africa the Songhai, Mali, and the Ghana empire these were Muslim empires, and Timbuktu the great learning center of the world. They didn't want any person, they wanted the strongest the wisest the best, they raped Africa of millions of people.

Have you read about the Spanish Inquisition, what was that all about it's all about the persecution of Jews and Muslims who ruled Spain for nearly 1000 years but they wanted to kick Muslims and Jews out of Spain, so when the Jews were punished and beaten and murdered, they left Spain, where did you go? They went into the Caribbean, into South America and they became plantation owners. This is why many Jewish people don't want us to talk about reparations, I'm not a hater it's the truth.

THE BREAKING OF THE BLACK WOMAN, SO SHE COULD PROGRAM THE NEXT GENERATION OF SLAVES.

Now, the breaking process is the same for the African as for the horse, same process. In other words, you must keep your eye and thoughts on the female. The female carried an important role. Their agenda was to keep an eye on the black female and her offspring. Pay little attention to the original slaves that were broken, the first few, their gold was for future generations.

Their fore if you break the female mother she will break the offspring, this was Will Lynch's concept, if you break the female mother, she will break her offspring in its early years of development, until it's old enough to work, then she will deliver it up to the slaveholder. Because her normal protective female tendencies would have been lost in the original breaking process. For example, take a female horse and an infant horse, two captured African males in their natural state, and a pregnant African woman with her infant offspring, breed the mayor and the stud until you have the desired offspring. Then you can turn the stud to freedom until you need him again.

Train the female horse, where she will eat out of your hand in turn, she will train her infant horse to eat out of your hand also. When it comes to breaking the uncivilized African, use the same process. Step up the pressure to do a complete reversal of the mind. Take the meanest and most restless African strip him of his clothes, in front of the remaining male Africans and females and the African infants, tar and feather him, tie each leg to a different horse face in opposite directions, set him afire, and beat both horses to tear him apart in front of the remaining Africans while they are looking at him.

The next step is to take a bullwhip, beat the remaining African males to the point of death, in front of the females, don't kill them, but put the fear of God in them. Now the breaking process for the African woman, run a series of tests on her, to see if she will submit to your desires, white man. Test her in every way, because she is the most important factor in good economics. If she shows any sign of resistance in submitting to your will, do not hesitate to use the bullwhip to extract the last bit of resistance out of her, take care not to kill her, for doing so, you spoil good economics.

when she is in complete submission, she will train her offspring, in their early years to submit to you, when they become of age. Understanding is the best thing; therefore, we shall go deeper into the area of the subject matter concerning what we have produced. Here, in this breaking process of the African female, at this point, we have now reversed the relationship. see what has happened? they have taken the strong African male and destroyed his image. while the women and children watching, so in the back of the woman's mind, black man you cannot protect us, you are not in the position to look after us.

In, her natural state she will have a strong dependency on that African man, she will raise her offspring to be dependent like she is, so in the natural state, the African woman and the child were dependent on the African male, nature provided for this type of balance. But we reverse nature by bullwhipping and pulling apart and burning a civilized African male, in front of the woman and children, we reversed nature, symbolizing we reversed what is natural we got rid of that black woman depending on that black man.

And God knows they did a good job because there is something sick when a black woman tells a black man I don't need you, the only thing, I need you and if you don't do that too well, I don't need you at all.

 her being left alone and unprotected with the male image destroyed the ordeal and causes her to move from her psychologically dependent state to a frozen independent state, in this frozen psychological state of independent state she will raise her male and female offspring in reversed roles. what are the results? You have the African woman out front and the African male behind and scared.

This is a perfect situation for us to have sound sleep and economics, before the breaking process we had to be on guard and alert at all times, for now out of frozen fear, his woman stands guard for us so we can sleep soundly. He cannot get past her early slave moving process he is a good tool now ready to be tied to a horse at the tender age of 16, he is broken in and ready for a long life of sound and efficient work, and the reproduction unit of a labor force.

In breaking, the uncivilized savage African by throwing the African female savage into a frozen sociological state of independence and by killing the protective male image, by creating a submissive dependent mine of the African male slave we have created a cycle that will turn on its axis. Unless a phenomenon occurs and re-shifts the position of the male and female slave. Here's what we must do, breed two African males with two African females, then take the African male away, like they are doing today, by incarceration and killing off the male, breed them, and make them have African children. Remove the African male away.

Keep them working and moving, let's say one African female has an African female child and the other bares an African male, both African females being without the influence of the African male will raise their offspring in a frozen independent sociological state, they will raise their offspring into reverse positions. The one with the female offspring will raise her daughter to be like herself, distrustful of the ability of the black male to be strong, and protective, and the one with the male offspring will raise her son to be frozen and in subconscious fear for his life, she will raise him to be mentally weak but physically strong.

This is called good sound long-range planning. Don't forget to pitch the young black male against the old black male, you must use dark-skinned slaves against light skin slaves versus dark skin slaves. use the female against male or male against female. You must have your white overseers distrust All Blacks it is necessary that your slaves trust and depend on only us, they must love, respect, and trust only us. Gentlemen, these are your keys to control, use them, have your wives and children use them at every opportunity, if used intensely for one year the slaves themselves will remain perpetually distrustful of each other. This was a small part of the Willie Lynch kit, which was sold to slave owners.

THE TRUTH WAS EXPOSED!

The Young Turks facebook.com

You, are asking us to talk about, the history of the south. What happens in Georgia? There were savages in Georgia, it was the ancestors of the white right-wingers. They were absolute savages, they murder people, lynched people, raped, and enslaved people. They took babies from their mothers and sold them as property. You want to talk about savages, your ancestors we're the biggest savages, the world has ever seen, and don't you dare call a black man a savage after you murdered him.

Don't you dare, do that, I'm so sick of African Americans being called violent when the world's worst violence was done to African people, not by them. You want to racist stereotype everything that doesn't fit your norm. Anywhere it would certainly fit white right-wingers in the South, who have hundreds of years as being savages. They snatched babies and sold them as property and then raped their mothers, you want to talk about stereotypes? I feel sorry for all of you that defend the confederacy that barbaric monstrosity, anyone who defends that is a savage.

That's why they don't want to teach American history in the public schools, that's why there's been a strong orchestrated effort to prevent the teaching of the true American history, that would include the south, right now because, hey God forbid, that your children learn about the real savages in this country's history.

Right, let's go ahead, and dehumanize people over their toenails, but let's also erase the part of our history that is dark, that's awful, but it's the truth. Do You know, what white right-wingers in the South did, for hundreds of years? At a lynching, they not only hung the person, but they also burned the person, and then they cut off their genitalia, and in the midst of all this, God IS MY JUDGE, you could look it up in the history books, they had a picnic around the body and then they would take-home piece of the charred body as memorabilia.

They would have their kids go pick pieces of the body off, and then after they did all of that, they had the temerity to call African people violent. No more, no more, do you get to call African people violent. So, if you are a white right-winger in the South don't cry, my beloved ancestors, your ancestors were not beloved, they were monsters. I said it because it's true, they shouldn't have done that.

RACE, RELIGION, AND RACISM

Dr. Frederick Price facebook.com

It, all started in the very beginning, when the preachers got into the league with the slave owners. The church, sanctioned slavery, the church, that's the only reason slavery could exist. Because, the church gave the slave owners the courage, to be able to exercise slavery and call themselves Christians.

How could a preacher? my God!! my God!! have mercy on the church, how could a preacher? minister of the gospel stand by and watch a   family offered up for sale on the auction block like you would a cow or sheep or goat, how could the church stand by silently, while that man, that father was bided for and sold to the highest bidder, while that wife with those little children standing around and clinging to the mother's tattered torn little garbage robes, that they gave them to ware, they watched that father go off and never have the possibility of seeing that man again. How could a preacher stand by, a man who claims to know God, and stand by and watch that?

What, is going on in our nation? we have to deal with this issue of race and we got to deal with it now. From, a standpoint of truth and from the standpoint of the word of God, because the Bible says things about it that the church has not lived out, that's why and the answer I believe is in the word and the spirit and must be modeled by the people of God before anybody else will ever be able to see that this is also something that has to be evidenced in the church.

Not, just that Jesus is a healer, not just that Jesus is a provider, not just that Jesus is a way maker, but Jesus is a reconciler of ethnic discord and ethnic hatred and the divisions, that have kept men and women apart and one of the reasons, in the United States of America that this festering has continued to occur is because of this issue of race and here's something you must understand as a child of God as a man or woman of God. I'm talking especially to preachers in pulpits both black and white race, the people ask me, so many times to get involved in racial discussions will you come and talk about race, when will you come? No, it's because I will not debate race. After all, the race is a historical lie.

Race, in its current 20th and 21st-century understanding, when I say race, I mean what we mean when we dialogue about race when they talk about race in politics when we talk about race on television, we talk about the race between black men and white men, black women and white women in America. Race in its current 20th and 21st century in America is a white invention. You have never seen what's happening in America, the way it's happening today and it is because there are things, that must be dealt with in truth and you and I as Christians, black or white have agreed that the word is truth, have we not? and if so, then we have something to do, because as I said, in its current 20th 21st-century understanding, it is a white invention, it is a product of the western predominantly European imperialistic and colonial system of subjugation.

Race is not in any way, shape, or form a divine biblical or even remotely Christian concept. I'm going to say that again race is not in any way shape or form a divine meaning, God didn't come up with it not a biblical or even a remotely Christian concept, how can you say that and you're just being too ethereal. So, what do you want to talk about, well here's the point, race is not even a biblical concept, and therefore the mere entertaining of the seduction to debate it is an exercise in futility that is destined for failure?

You see, what do you mean, it can't produce any long-lasting results, just pay attention, we've been debating race for hundreds of years, whatever happens, it's short-lived. Why the issue of race is not a matter of truth, it's an invention. From the biblical standpoint, there is one race and that race is human and within that race, there are distinct ethnicities, the whole idea of the race it's a western concept because the United States of America has been the predominant political system affecting the world, that invention has infected the entire globe. You travel to other nations, people talking about race you hear them talking about ethnic discord or tribal discord, not racial discord.

Why? because the fact of the matter is, you cannot in your Declaration of Independence, you cannot write and pin the words we hold these truths to be self-evident that all men are created equal, that they are endowed by their creator with certain inalienable rights and that, among these are life, liberty and the pursuit of happiness, you cannot write in your Declaration of Independence that we hold these truths to be self-evident, that all men are created equal and then enslave another man and go to bed with a good Christian conscience unless you have first reduced that other man to be subhuman to be another race other than you.

So, the whole concept of race is the dehumanization of nonwhite people in America, so that the good unilluminated Christian conscience, could enslave a man of another color and still say we hold these truths to be self-evident, that all men are created equal because the one I enslaving is not a man he is not my species, oh, he or she, is another race, therefore I am justified in what I do to them because they're not on my level. Now that is the historical LIE that has been perpetuated in the western world it has been adopted by the Christian concepts, but it is not biblical. I am appalled, quite frankly to hear otherwise spiritual men, fathers in the Kingdom of God, who are sticklers for every other aspect of the accuracy of the word but continue to preach a distinction in the race.

If, you are a white preacher if you're a black preacher. I want to say this clearly to you, there is no such thing as race in the Kingdom of God, there is one race and that race is human. The term race is only mentioned one time in the entirety of the word of God and that is in the book of Zachariah Chapter 9 verse 6, the book of Zechariah chapter 9 verse 6 is the only place where race is referred to and their race is not being referred to in the distinction of any kind of color or dehumanization, there the word that is translated race from Hebrew into English is the Hebrew word Manzar, which means bastard and it is meaning from the Jewish culture of an individual has a Jewish father and a non-Jewish mother.

It is a mixed racial settle Ashdod meaning people with Jewish fathers and non-Jewish mothers it is not talking about a difference in color or species that's the only time the word race is used in the scripture and it is not a reference to color distinction. Acts: Chapter 17, Paul is preaching in verse 25, he is not served with men's hands as though he needed anything since he gives life to all, breath and all things and he has made from one blood every nation of men, to dwell on the face of the earth, and one Blood that determines race, not color and the boundaries of their dwelling. God has made all men from one blood, so it is the blood that determines race, not color.

Man; is the only one of gods creations, who has been ignorant enough to accept the lie that a distinction in color denotes a distinction in a race. You, don't do that with birds, they're the same species, if they're difficult, you don't do it with horses, they're the same species, you, don't do it with dogs somehow, with men we have bought the lie, the unbiblical lie and we wonder why this continues?

It; continues, because when you debate a lie, based on an erroneous premise, even if you win the argument, you've got no closer to the truth. What are you saying? he has made, the Bible says, from one blood, he has made all nations, this is the Bible. Preachers, how dare you, get in your church and talk to people about loving other races there's only one, and until the church accepts it and begins to preach it, we cannot expect the world to change their mind about anything. he has made, from one blood all nations, that word nations, that is the Greek word ethnos for which we get our English word ethnic. So, all men are of the same race, they are of different ethnicities, and ethnicity is diversity, not race.

now once again you're making a distinction without a difference. No, you must understand, that is the historical lie of the western European imperialist and colonialist world, is we have reduced you to another race; so that we can justifiably with Christian conscience take advantage of you and that is intelligible in the culture and until somebody digs up the historical lie, and says here's the lie that you perpetuate, we are destined to continue to repeat it.

YOU BETTER, SHUT YOUR WHITE MOUTH.

@BROTHERBENX.facebook.com

I, think back on the African American people, in America. I, think how they were taken against their wills, put in the belly of ships, brought over here beat, cussed many of them died in the guts of those ships, some died and were thrown overboard. They were pulled from families in Africa, you are never heard of a gut-wrenching song until, you hear a black person sing, one of those old black Negros spirituals, nobody nos.

I; have never had that experience. When you've experienced hell, it comes out in the voice, I, said when you experience hell, it comes out in the voice. If, you're one of those people, that you got a problem with black people or whatever, you better shut your mouth. Cause they're gods people, you better shut your white mouth.

I, know some of you were raised in the deep south, you were raised by prejudiced people and bigoted People. You, better get that out of your system, you better get it out of your system. Because it will cause you, to suffer right along with those masters. it will cause you to suffer right along with them. A lot of people do not understand or do not want to, you have to pay for the deeds done in your body before you leave this earth.

These, are God's people and me, know that there's wicked in white races and black races, God knows what happen to the black race, how they end up over here and God is going to reimburse the black people for all their troubles and all their labor? And just like he (God) will pay the Africans for the things done against them, the ones that committed the atrocities against the African people. There, is another Ole saying, payday is coming after a while. Don't, think you live, and then you die, no. The; the bible says, after death and then the judgment, all must stand before God, and give an account of the deeds done in our bodies.

"IF YOU AREN'T RACIST, YOU'RE A MIRACLE"

Ms. Jane Elliott

Any, white person, who was born, raised, and schooled in the United States of America; if you aren't a racist, you are a miracle, either that, or you decided to educate yourself. Because education in this country is about, white is right, Browns alright, Black's got to stand back, yellow is mellow, but whites we educate in a way, that says, white males, have done all the adventures, have made all the adventures; have done all the discovering that have been made, everything that is good and has been accomplished according to social studies, which is anti-social studies by white males, it's a lie.

But we can do that, to maintain the myth of white superiority. The myth of race has to be maintained at all costs in this country, because if white people have to give up the color of their skin as being something that makes them perfect, what do they have left if we start teaching the truth about history if we start teaching about Nile valley contributions to civilization, it will change the way we conduct ourselves in the classroom it will have to! Columbus didn't discover America you can't discover a place where people are already living, but we celebrate that every October it's a LIE.

We, need to stop telling the myths and start telling the truth. If some person says I am not a racist, some of my best friends are black, then you say, name one! or this one, I don't see color and when someone says to me, I don't see color, I say I, knew that if you saw color, you wouldn't dye your hair that way or I, say if you saw color, you wouldn't wear that shirt with those pants, I believe that you don't see color, it's an attempt to deny skin color.

 It's, alright for you to see someone kind of pink, that's OK for them, I don't mind and I, suspect that you don't mind being seen the color you are, you have a right to be what you are and until people in this country and people in this world get it into their heads, that the first modern human beings evolved on this earth were black women, they evolved in sub-Saharan Africa about 280,000 years ago and every human being on the face of the earth today runs the app of having the memory of those black women's genetic structure in their genes, now we don't want to admit that, but that's the way it is.

As people, moved farther and farther from the equator, their bodies produce less and less melanin, so their hair, their skin, and their eyes got lighter, as they moved into the east, they ate a lot of fish and a lot of vegetables, so their skin took on a different tone.

A man worked in a supermarket, he, was head of the produce department and they had lots of oranges, that they couldn't sell. So, he would take them home and his wife would feed their children, oranges and orange juice, as you had never seen in your life. There, the children began to have an orange cast on their skin, and the wife, though they had some kind of a liver problem. So, she took them to the doctor.

And, the doctor asked, what are you feeding these kids? the wife answered lots of oranges, she said stop it, if you want them to stop being orange. Now, if you think that skin color isn't anything other than the body's natural reaction to the natural environment, get over it.

 So, if all white people are racist, can they be re-programed? of course, they can, it's called education. That's, what an "educator" does. The word educator comes from the root word "dux duce" which means lead, the prefix, E which means out, the suffix, A-T-E which means the act of, and the suffix, O-R which means One who does!" an educator, is engaged in the act of leading people out of ignorance.

we need to stop believing the myth, because education in this country is indoctrination, and it takes us from the ages of five to the age of 18 to thoroughly indoctrinate people. So, they will believe in the myth of white superiority, and it is a myth, right now you can't do that while you're teaching that Columbus discovered America, there were black people on this continent 4000 years before Columbus was born. We teach black history in school as though it started with slavery.

If you are a white person, in all actuality, you are a faded black person, when different people moved farther from the equator and that's the only reason why their skin is lighter, that's all, any white person is. There's only one race and that race is human. The same black women 10,000 years ago that's when the human race began with Black women. whether you like it or not, we are all cousins, make no mistake about this, we are all 30th to 50th cousins because we all have the same black great, great, great grandmother genes in our blood.

Back 300,000 to 500,000 years ago, we all came from those black women. So, get over the idea. So, if you think, that white makes you superior. There's, only one race and that race is human. How long do you think that the idea of race has been around? The 1400s, started with the Spanish inquisition before that, the race was not a problem, but they wouldn't find out that they were killing people who were of their religious beliefs but they couldn't tell what their religion was by looking at them so they had to find another way to identify those they were going to kill.

So, they set the bar, on skin color. We have also been indoctrinated with the myth of white superiority. We've got pictures, of the baby Jesus, who looks like the little Pillsbury doughboy, he didn't look like the Pillsbury doughboy, that's true and it says in the Bible that Jesus had hair like lamb's wool and feet of bronze, here's what you can do, educate yourself, the schools want to do it, they don't want you to know the truth, they can't afford to have blacks knowing the truth, but what you have to realize is within thirty years, whites will have become a numerical minority in the United States of America.

Now, blacks and other people of color, have to stop playing defense and start playing offense. I think that part of the responsibility that we as a black community need to take on is educating ourselves and preparing ourselves absolutely yeah educate yourself and your children when they come home from school, spouting this crap that they've learned in school you will have to say, here look at this, 's what happens, there is one race, the human race.

HOW WHITE AND JEWISH PEOPLE, GOT SO RICH OFF PEOPLE OF COLOR AND COTTON

Minister Lewis Farrakhan

The secret relationship of the Jewish people goes heavily into the horrors of the transatlantic slave trade. I, have never been to Elmina castle at Cape Coast in Ghana? 15 years ago, on the doors of the castle, you would see a Star of David, if you go there now, they have taken it down. Because they did not want you to understand the connection that they have to the transatlantic slave trade. Do you know that many white people don't know why you are in the condition that you are in?

Have, you ever stopped and asked yourself, why? immigrants could come to this country, and in a few years, run right past us and we've been here all our lives. Is, it because we are inferior, or is it because the architecture of white supremacy and it is nobbily was at work keeping you in a position that you will never rise from? Well, In the Jewish encyclopedia, I, quote that the cotton plantations in many parts of the South, were wholly in the hands of the Jews, and as a consequence slavery found its advocates among them.

 It wasn't just gentiles, these were the people, in fact in Brazil it is said on a Jewish holiday, no slaves could be bought or sold because it was a holiday. So, what does that tell you about slavery in Brazil? 80 million Africans in Brazil were brought there as slaves. Siblings, the horror of the transatlantic slave trade was real, and how the South became the leader in the production of cotton.

 The Mississippi Delta was the greatest cotton-producing part of the south on the planet earth. Cotton was then, what oil is now, the largest producer of oil in the world are the rich ones and the strategic interests of America. this means, that for them to rule, they have to link with where the oil is coming from and take it or maneuver it to get it to where it is needed. But they must have oil, In the time of slavery, it was cotton and it's interesting, that the cotton would come down the Mississippi, New Orleans to the gulf, from Biloxi Mississippi, and mobile and, the cotton would come down and go up to New York.

Jewish, people in the South, would make connections with the Jewish people in the north. They, were masters of the needle trades and had their brothers also in the South taking the lint from the cotton and producing cloth through weaving, but these were Jewish people owning the land they were the majority, they were the merchants, they were the traders they knew how to hook up with their brethren in the north and they would send raw cotton to the mills in England in Manchester, Leeds and Bristol and the British would turn it into a cloth and then sell it all over the world.

So, from cotton, the South became rich, from cotton it fueled the industrial revolution in the north, from cotton the Rothschild became rich, from cotton the Lehman Brothers became rich, from cotton in Alabama, then moved to New York and Wall Street. The areas where the cotton was produced, were North Carolina, Tennessee, South Carolina, Georgia, Alabama, Mississippi, Arkansas, Louisiana, and Texas. In the Mississippi delta, let me tell you brothers and sisters in Mississippi, brothers, and sisters even right to this moment some of our brothers and sisters are still in slavery in Mississippi, Alabama, and Louisiana.

The Cotton-Pickin Truth Still on The Plantation is a movie, a black woman is talking, she just got out of slavery in the 60s, and she talked about how they raped her mother, she was five years old and how they raped her. This is from her lips. people on large tracts of land in Mississippi way out in the rural district. But people are sitting there, working there, living there, with nothing. This woman says she lived in a barn, she had no place to lay her head, she was sleeping on hay, she would eat crickets, sometimes there would be a worm and she would bite a piece and give a piece of the worm to her children, anything that came in front of them, they had to kill it to eat, this wasn't in 1850 or 1860 this was in 1960.

The research society researched it. While you were working on the plantation, you couldn't buy from anybody but the owner of the store on the plantation. You would pick the cotton and you would get your bacon or whatever you needed from the store, and they would write it down in a book. But, by the time the harvest season had come, you go back to get your pay, you find the manipulation of the books, that you still owe money. So, you had to stay on the plantation.

They, force black people back on the plantation. Look, from these little stores, they became rich. Because everything an African person on the plantation needed, they had to get it from the store. see while we were in slavery, they gave you a little something, but now look at this 1863 was the Emancipation Proclamation, right? 1865 we were supposed to be free, according to the 13, 14, and 15th amendments

Something went wrong, because, after 12 years from 1865 to 1877, white folks said quote if the negro's leave the land, we don't have anybody to work the land, that's how we get our money, so we had to find a way to put the Africans back on the land. Listen, to this, it's called the compromise of 1877 this compromise can easily be listed among the most significant events in African American history. The country was in an uproar over the disputed election of 1876 involving presidential rivals Rutherford B Hayes and Samuel J Tilden, but the root of the conflict was once again the fate of the African man.

Since emancipation, the north had placed troops in the South, to keep the whites from putting the freed blacks back into plantation slavery, but after 13 years of this so-called reconstruction. Whites all over the country, North and South had grown tired and angry over fighting each other over the rights of their ex-slaves. Both parties, republican and Democrat convened at the Wormley Hotel in Washington DC, to attempt to resolve the conflict and on February 26th, 1877, a deal was struck, it would profoundly affect the course of history for African People in America.

All agreed, that the country's needs for cotton required that Africans, be returned to virtual slavery and assigned to permanent political, social, and economic inferiority are you with me know, they made a deal in the Wormley Hotel, then we had to be put back on the plantation, a Jewish man by the name of Levy, who was in Congress was the spokesperson, that went back to Congress to sell the idea of putting Africans back on the plantation.

THE GAME OF MONOPOLY, EXPLAINS RACISM AND SLAVERY.

Dr. Fredrick Price and Kevin Goldstar

After the civil war in 1865 when we were emancipated, we were supposed to get 40 acres and a mule. That's true, I said that is true, that's not a figment, that is actually what was going to happen. It was documented and written down. And, then they killed Abraham Lincoln. And your next president that came up vetoed the idea and we were emancipated with nothing.

But over the holidays, I had an opportunity to put it into operation. I think everybody in America knows about the game called a monopoly. Well, anyway, if you know anything about monopoly, every player starts with $1500. Well, I wanted to play the advocate, The African advocate. So, we played monopoly. The other night and I didn't take any money. I wanted to take the place of the Africans that were emancipated in 1865, who did not get the 40 acres or mule.

And so, I took nothing. I survived a few times around the board, but I couldn't buy anything. And, it was very soon, I was out of the game. Now, you would say that is unfair to have somebody sit down at a table and play monopoly and not give them the $1,500 to start with. But that's what this country did with our people when they emancipated us. And then have the audacity, the unmitigated gall to wonder why we don't do better? And you started with 1,500, And we started with nothing.

And they know that if we ever let these African people get equality, they will take over, and they will be on top of everything. If, I right now, decided I wanted to play monopoly with you, and for 400 rounds of playing monopoly I didn't allow you to have any money, I didn't allow you to have anything on the board. I didn't allow for you to have anything, and then we played another 50 rounds of monopoly, and everything that you gained, and you earned while you're playing that round of monopoly was taken from you that was Tulsa that was Rosewood those were places where we built black economic wealth.

Where we were self-sufficient, where we owned our stores, where we owned our property, and they burn them to the ground 450 years. So, for 400 rounds of monopoly you do not get to play at all, not only you did not get to play, but you also have to play on the behalf of the person that you're playing against.

You have to play and make money for them; you have to turn it over to them. So, then for 50 years you finally get a little bit and you're allowed to play, and every time that they don't like the way that you're playing you're doing something to be self-sufficient, they burn your game, they burn your cards, they burn your monopoly money, and then finally at the release and the onset of that they allow you to play and they say to you catch-up, now at this point in the game the only way for you to catch-up in the game is if the person shares the wealth.

Then, there is psychological warfare against you, then they say you are an equal opportunity hire. So, if I played, 400 rounds of monopoly with you and I had to give you every dime that I made, and then for 50 years every time that I played if you didn't like what I did you got your burn it's like they did in Tulsa, as they did in Rosewood, how can you win, you can't win, the game is fixed. So, when they say, why did you burn down the community, why do you burn down the neighborhood. It's not ours, we don't own anything.

Trevor Noah said it so beautifully last night, there's a social contract that we all have to live by, if you steal or if I steal then the person who is the authority comes in and they fix the situation. But the person that comes to fix the situation is killing us. The social contract is broken, those people don't care about burning the football Hall of Fame or a Target, they don't care, you broke the contract.

I, give up you broke the contract for 400 years we played your game and build your wealth you broke the contract when we built our wealth again on our own by our bootstraps they turned, and you dropped bombs on us when we built it in Rosewood, and you came in and you slaughtered us you broke the contract they do not care about your Target. You can burn it to the ground, it still would not be enough, and they are lucky black people are looking for quality and not revenge.

WHAT HAPPENED, WHEN THE SLAVES WERE FREED

Weird History facebook.com/

American school children are taught, that slaves in confederate states were freed when Abraham Lincoln issued the Emancipation Proclamation, on September 22nd, 1862. While true, the reality of actually freeing those slaves was far more complicated. Today we're going to take a look at what happened on plantations when the slaves were freed. you would think that once freed, the slaves would get off the plantations as fast as humanly possible.

But in his autobiography, Booker T. Washington mentioned, that many ex-slaves, especially older ones, decided to stay. Although free, these ex-slaves typically made deals with their former masters to work for pay. According to Washington, one by one the older slaves began to wander from the slave quarters, back to the big house to have a whispered conversation with their former owners as to the future. Thomas Ruling was only nine when he and his fellow slaves learned of their emancipation. He thought freedom would mean his family would now live a life like their former master.

But instead, the family chose to stay on the plantation for another two years. Rutledge along with his brother and sister finally left the plantation in 1865. They went to live with the family in Nashville. He later attended the Fisk Free Colored School which eventually became Fisk University. In her 1909 book, memories of Childhood Slavery Days, ex-slave Annie Albertan wrote of her own experiences with emancipation. Annie recalled that when the news reached the Alabama plantation she worked on, every slave who wasn't feeble or sickly left immediately.

Some of these younger, healthier ex-slaves even immediately joined the Union Army however, because their mother had run away, Annie and her younger sisters stayed behind under the care of their mistress. This may not have been the act of charity it appears to be. This same mistress tried to talk her husband into not telling, the slaves about their freedom and then made the feeble and sickly slaves who remained on the plantation work the fields. After, the crops were planted some plantation owners, asked their ex-slaves to sign contracts, guaranteeing they would work the crops until January.

 They would then be divided at the fall harvest for payment. Such a deal is mentioned in the Reverend Irving E. Lowry's Book Life on the Old Plantation in Antebellum Days, or A Story Based on Facts. Lowery said his ex-master tried to convince the slaves to sign the deals by making a long speech in which he reminded them that he wasn't a bad guy. The plantation owner pointed out that he never put an overseer over them, never employed bloodhounds, and never separated a mother from her child, nor husband from his wife. He also told them that they were welcome to stay on this plantation as long as they like and that any mistreatment, they had experienced on the plantation was their fault and not his. Although that argument might sound meager to us, all but one ex-slave signed the contract.

Charles Hayes owned a plantation 16 miles north of Louisville Kentucky, like many slave owners, Hays at first chose not to tell his slaves about emancipation at all. However, after a few days, he relented out of fear of being arrested. According to ex-slave Harry Smith in his 1891 book, 50 years of slavery in the United States of America, Hayes broke the news by saying, "I am about to tell you something I never expected to be obliged to tell you in my life. it is this one and all, woman, men, and children belonging to me, you are free to go where you please." Smith also noted that, at the same time, Hays was cursing Lincoln's name and exclaiming that if Lincoln were there, he'd kill him for taking his slaves away.

However, after Hayes cooled down, he gave the entire plantation access to his whiskey stash and threw what sounds like a pretty decent party. It was described as a great jubilee in which the ex-master and all the ex-slaves got drunk together. Smith recalls that everyone was cheering Abraham Lincoln, but Hayes was way too drunk to notice. By nightfall, the revelers had broken into song and dance and kept it up until morning.

According to the civil war diary of James T. Ayres, Charles Hayes was far from being the only master who tried to hide the news of emancipation from his slaves. Ayers was a union recruiter who went into the South to enlist newly freed men into the Union Army. Things being as they were, he also often found himself as the person to inform the ex-slaves that they were, in fact, now free. In his diary entry for May 7th, 1864, Ayres recorded spreading the word about emancipation to a group of four ex-slaves on a plantation near Huntsville, AL. He accomplished this by showing them a broadside that featured an illustration of freed slaves on one side and a two-sentence version of the Emancipation Proclamation on the other.

Ayres states the four men agreed to enlist, so he told them to gather the things, and he promised he would protect them. When they were confronted by their ex-master, Ayres drew his revolver, and sounding much like a hero in an action movie, calmly told the man, "I shall not hurt a hair of your head, Sir if you be quiet. But I have come for your slaves, and your slaves I'll have." It is believed that Ayres recruited hundreds of black soldiers to the Union cause and spread the word of emancipation to thousands before his death in September of 1865.

According to his 1901 autobiography, Up from Slavery the first day of freedom at the Virginia plantation where Booker T. Washington was born started with a simple, solemn meeting.

The meeting was then followed by a reading of the Emancipation Proclamation by a government official, and the news was initially quite well received, by the now-former slaves. Washington recalled that the master's entire family had gathered on the veranda of the house. He got the impression that they were sad, not because of the loss of property, but rather because they were, in many ways, very close to some of the ex-slaves who would now be leaving. He recalled his mother kissing her children while tears of joy ran down her cheeks.

According to Washington for some minutes, there was great rejoicing and thanksgiving and wild scenes of ecstasy, but there was no feeling of bitterness. There was pity among the slaves, for our former owners. Once the initial joy passed, however, many of the ex-slaves began to feel anxiety over what freedom would mean. Washington observed, "The great responsibility of being free of having charge of themselves, of having to think and plan for themselves and their children seem to take possession of them." He noted that some of the slaves were 70 or 80 years old and had no strength with which to earn a living. According to 1908 generously titled Memoirs of Samuel spot for Clement Relating Interesting Experiences in Days of Slavery and Freedom, Clément's ex-master, Basswood Ward, informed him and the other slaves on Ward's plantation of their freedom by reading to them from the newspaper, Spottford offered recall that when Mr. and Mrs. Ward came out of the house, he was holding a newspaper and she was crying.

They walked to the front of the steps, and he said, "Men and women, you are as free as the birds that fly in the air." Ward then raised the paper and read from it. He informed the ex-slaves that Lee had surrendered to Grant and the southern confederacy was at an end. He then offered to pay them and to stay and help reap the crops. The offer was accepted by all but one man. known only as Uncle Fendel, the man was concerned that the rebels might pick up the fight again and revoke their freedom There is somebody who has been around the block once or twice. Thomas almond Ashby was 17 years old when he watched his father inform the family slaves on their Front Royal, Virginia plantation that they were all now free. In his 1914 memoir The Valley Campaigns, Ashby recalled that his father told the ex-slaves that he had no further control over them and that in the future, he would pay them for their services based on wage rates established by the community.

 He told them that if they wish to stay in as employ, they could do so as long as they desired, but that if any of them wish to seek out a new home, you wouldn't try to stop them from making a change. The elder Ashby further assured the now-freed people that he had nothing but a friendly desire to see them do well and be happy bring and he urged them to cultivate habits of thrift and industry. He believed hard work would make them useful citizens and earn them self-respect, which is some pretty ironic advice coming from a slave owner.

According to Ashby, it took several years before all of the ex-slaves had finally left the plantation. One woman known only as aunt Susan seems to take Ashby's advice about thrift to heart. After saving up three years' worth of money she earned taking in the wash and doing light work, she acted to buy a neat little house in the city. Juneteenth is also known as Emancipation Day or Freedom Day is an official holiday in the state of Texas and an unofficial American holiday that commemorates June 19th, 1865, on that date Union General Gordon Granger read from the federal proclamation that slavery was over in the state of Texas.

While the Emancipation Proclamation had ended slavery in the confederacy more than two years earlier, it took some time for the news to reach all parts of the war-torn states. Granger's proclamation guaranteed absolute equality of personal rights and rights of property between former masters and slaves. It also declared that the connection between master and slave was officially replaced by that between employer and hired labor during the late 19th century, Juneteenth was primarily celebrated by the black community. However, the civil rights movement in the 1950s and 60s led to a renewed interest in the holiday at a wider level maybe it became an official holiday, in the state of Texas, and in the 21st century has become a widely recognized day to celebrate black historical achievements and encourage respect and pride in all cultures.

THE BOOTLESS MAN"

Dr. Martin L. King facebook.com

The fact that negros are black, white America must-see,
that no other ethnic group has been a slave on American
soil. That is one thing that other immigrant groups haven't
had to face. The other thing is that the color of their skin
became a stigma American Society made the negroes'
color a stigma. America freed the slaves in 1863, through
the emancipation proclamation of Abraham Lincoln, but
gave the slaves no land, nothing, in reality, to get started
on. At the same time, America was giving away millions
of acres of land in the West and the Midwest.

This meant that there was a willingness to give the white
peasants from Europe an economic base. And yet it
refused to give its black peasants from Africa who came
here involuntarily, in chains, and had worked free for 244
years any kind of economic base, and so emancipation for
the negro, was freedom to hunger. It was freedom to the
winds and rains of heaven. It was freedom without food to

eat or land to cultivate and therefore it was freedom and famine at the same time.

 And when white Americans tell the negro to lift himself by his bootstraps, they don't look over the legacy of slavery and segregation. I believe we ought to do all we can and seek to lift ourselves by our bootstraps. But, it's a cruel gesture to say to a bootless man that he ought to lift himself by his straps. And many Negroes, by the thousands and millions, have been left bootless as a result of all of these years of oppression and as a result of a society that deliberately made his color a stigma and something worthless and degrading.

"BLACK HISTORY IN TWO MINUTES"

Henry Louis Gates, Jr.

Long, before Abraham Lincoln, signed the homestead act of 1862. Which offered settlers up to 160-acre parcels of free land. Free, African Americans had been cultivating, land and establishing homes in the Midwest. Helping to set the stage, for the nation's western expansion. The Northwest Territory, the area that we now refer to as the heartland of the United States, Wisconsin, Ohio, Michigan, and Minnesota was settled as the United States' first frontier. It was established as a free territory, without slavery.

Clearing the land was arduous, it was a heavily forested part of the United States, and it required chopping down trees and plowing. African Americans were active participants in that process of really making what would become the nation's bread basket. African Americans, very much understood to have any semblance of true freedom, that they were going to have to be land owners, despite the tremendous work of early African American pioneers.

White Americans took great efforts to ensure that these black farmers felt unwelcome in the new frontier. By 1851 both Indiana and Illinois had passed laws prohibiting, African Americans from settling there. By 1860, the states of the Northwest Territory would be dotted with 330 rural settlements that free black farmers called home. Over time they would lose their autonomy through voting restrictions, violence, theft, and exclusionary antiblack laws. One, of the most tragic aspects of settling the frontier, is that over time these territories developed a series of laws and practices that allowed for African Americans, who were free to be sold back into slavery.

We begin, to see a steady decrease in the number of black farmers, it accelerates during the depression, in part, because of the economic catastrophe. But, also because of how the federal government then props up large white land owners and does not provide the same protections and assistance to smaller black farmers. Currently, less than 2% of farmers are African American, despite having this steep and long history of agricultural labor and farming in the United States.

AMERICA'S BIG WHITE SECRET

@1MillionAfricans: Trilogy

America, is one of the wealthiest countries in the world, but the question is how did it accumulate its wealth? This is a nation founded on genocide, and built on the backs of slaves. So, we started with a racial problem. we tried to eliminate one entire race and then, we used another race to build this country quickly, as a new country, into a world power. This, the country never would have the wealth, if it had not had slavery, for a couple of hundred years. But I say to white people, look you didn't do it, yeah that's right, we didn't have anything to do with slavery. But because of slavery, immigrants came here. America was already built with the blood and sweat of my ancestors.

So, you got what you got, because your fathers, gave us what they gave us. One mistake is often made is showing how the South, the confederacy acquired their wealth off the back of our ancestors, and even then, it's reduced to just a few slave owners, who saw the real benefits of channel slavery of blacks benefited the South. But just as much, it benefited the north and all of America and its many European immigrants. America's economic structure was propelled by its dominant export sold throughout the world, cotton. This, one crop provided over half of all U.S. export earnings. By, 1840 60% of the world's cotton was grown, picked, and labored over for free by our ancestors.

These, plantation owners were racking in money, accumulating great wealth, and never having to pay one dime to their laborers. The north was just as involved, the north developed a variety of businesses, that provided services to the slave south, like textile factories, insurance companies, shippers, and cotton brokers, but it doesn't stop at the slave owner or the businesses that provided the services to the slave system. Banks, yes, bankers on Wall Street made millions. Selling, goods to the South, along with giving loans and creating banks to finance southern plantations and much of the same wealth they still have today.

Let me give you some examples, JP Morgan and Chase Bank admitted that between the years of 1831 to 1865, two of their predecessor banks, Citizens Bank Louisiana accepted 13,000 slaves as collateral on loans that slave masters defaulted. One, of the more successful banking families that built much of their wealth on the slave trade, was the Brown family. comely known as the Brown Brothers and Harriman company. Which is the oldest and largest private investment bank. The Brown Brothers owned hundreds of slaves; this family dominated the cotton industry. They made a huge fortune by lending millions to southern planters and cotton brokers; another portion of their wealth came from renting and the sales of slave ships.

They were sold to slave merchants. They served as one of the most important sources of capital in foreign exchange in the US economy. Wachovia bank recently acquired by Wells Fargo also profited heavily off this cruel system. Mayor Rothschild, a German banker and the founder of the Rothschild banking dynasty, which is believed to have become the wealthiest family in human history, made enormous gains by using our ancestors as collateral. The insurance industry, also saw great benefits from slavery companies, like AIG, Aetna, and New York life was the forerunners in this industry.

This, is also very important to note, that these same plantation owners and business owners, would donate large sums of their wealth to train their children and the next generation on containing the wealth. For example, Harvard was built by giving large amounts of money, given by Isaac Royall, a plantation owner in the Caribbean islands of Antigua, who made a massive fortune off of his many sugar plantations. Yale was able to build its famous library and establish its prestigious scholarship program. Princeton by the mid-1700s many of its students were sons of plantation owners.

Brown University, named after the famous slave owner banker the brown brothers, a large portion of this campus was built with slave labor, and these are just a few of the many institutions that were built with slave money. See these men will be looked at as great businessmen, and philanthropists, but in actuality, they were training and educating the next generation that, would take over their plantations and their businesses and even become government officials, responsible for creating laws regulations, and policies that would keep Africans fighting for human rights and access to the stolen wealth for decades after slavery.

 Blacks have fought against unequal education, which is a sure way of ensuring wealth disparities. Grandfather clauses, prevent us from affecting government, in ways that could transfer wealth. Land grants, free land in Iowa and Nebraska issued from the government, that blacks were restricted from, the black codes, housing restrictions, redlining and FDA guarantee loans, predatory bank lending, convict leasing, which utilized African labor but does not transfer the wealth. I wish, that I could say, this wealth disparity in America was isolated only in America. But it's not, all the wealth that was generated helped to make Britain great. So, called the British Empire, all of this came from links to this modern discussion around inequality, and the huge gap between the nations, not only in terms of Britain and Europe but also in the rest of the world and particularly Africa and the Caribbean.

This is the same scenario across every colonized land today, as a people, we fight for the confederate flags to come down, we even fight for people to stop using the word Nigger, or other forms of bigotry, to not be used, but we've been duped into believing that it's foolish to continue to fight for reparations. Many, of us don't recognize the direct ties of the past and the wealth that is carried into today our ancestors were forced to invest in this economy without ever receiving a return. Unlike Jews, reparations were never paid to slaves or their descendants to help balance out this unjustified wealth.

Understand, that the reason my ancestors were enslaved, was not even to be able to raise a slave flag. No, all of the killing, the torturing, dehumanizing, and inhumane treatment all boiled down to one reason wealth. It was all business understand that. I know that my brother Martin did. At the same time that America refused to give the Negros any land through an act of Congress, our government was giving away millions of acres of land in the West and the Midwest. Which, meant that it was willing to undergird its white pleasant from Europe.

But, not only did they give the land, they built land grant colleges, with government money to teach them how to farm, not only that, they provided county agents to help their expertise in farming, not only they provided low-interest-rate loans so that they could mechanize their farms, not only that these people are receiving millions of dollars in federal subsidy not to farm, and they are the very people telling the black man that he ought to lift himself by his bootstraps.

THE FACTS!!

Shannon Sharpe

It's difficult, to discuss race, with white people. If you talk all the way real about America and try to have an open and honest dialogue conversation with white America, then it would go to the fact it would tear down the very foundation of the very fabric, on which America was built. America was not built on freedom; America was built on racism and the backbone, the lifeblood of the economy of America was built on the backs of slaves. That is a fact and racism is so ingrained in America because from the very first time when you brought those slaves over in 1619 you had someone to look down on.

America robbed him of his given name, you robbed him of his dignity, you robbed him of his humanity you told him he was less than you treated him as less than, and then somehow, you say that America is the land of the free, home of the brave. you got 250 years of free labor. 250, because, let me tell you how this works!! When you hire someone to do a job, eighter, you couldn't do the job or you don't want to do the job, so which is it? As America was thriving, who was doing the work? not only were they working in the field they were taking care of your kids before they could take care of their own, so this notion that America, white people say we did the work, no you didn't.

We, have to look at the greatest purveyor of racism, and violence as the American white man. No, a race of people has suffered more on American soil than the African, no one to this day, so you had 250 years of free labor. You could argue the Native Americans were not enslaved for 250 years. They were just murdered and took their homes. The white man has been stealing and looting since the inception of America. So, when you talk, openly and honestly, about what they did to the American black, and some people say that was so long ago. that's ingrained. years and years, you don't have any income. So, Great grandfathers, had sons and sons and sons, that had nothing they had no wealth, while the white man were passing it down from generation to generation, The slave owner, passed down his father was a slave owner, see how that wealth kept going down from generation to generation.

But the blacks, always having to start from scratch, because you know that some of the slaves couldn't read, a lot of these guys, they couldn't read and if they catch you, you would be beaten or even killed. So, it took us a long time and those were the ones that happened to be the few that overcame. So, if we have an open dialog, about what America is and how America came to be how do you tell the story without telling about the American slave and his significant role in American history, but they'll tell you about George Washington, George Washington had slaves, they will tell you about Thomas Jefferson, he had slaves, but he wrote the Declaration of Independence, and he even had children by Sally Hemming.

When she was only 14 years old, he took her across state lines, for illegal purposes, these are our founding fathers. So, if we tell the story of America in its totality honestly, white America can't deal with that still, because they want to feel that we discovered it. After all, we wanted a better way of life and we yadda yadda but that's not it and so you're going to have to rewrite history all those history books will have to be burned. Instead of sidebars and footnotes.

African America has to be featured very prominently; I think that America wants to do that? I have never sat down and had a conversation with a white man about race relations. No. because the first thing he wants to say is black-on-black crime. What about the crime in Chicago? You always want to shift the blame, I don't want to talk about, let's talk about this head-on let's talk about what you did, how you robbed pillaged looted the Native Americans of their land, and, how you enslave brought men and women to cultivate this land.

Cooking, miss Mary didn't do any cooking, who took care of the kids, she didn't take care of no kids, so stop it, if you want to tell the story we have to tell it in its totality that's too much history, over 400 years you don't want to rewrite that kind of history. It's, easy for some whites to talk about race, it's because they have accepted the part that the white man played in the shaping of America and the atrocities which he perpetrated against black America and the Native Americans on American soil.

The reason why blacks? Can talk about what happened to us. It's cathartic, for us because we're talking about what is happening and my grandmother did a lot, my grandmother had raised white kids and she would let them play with her kid because the black women would suckle the white children before they suckle their own.

So, if you want to tell the story, something called the Mississippi appendectomy, black women would go to get a procedure and the doctors would give them a hysterectomy. If we are going to tell the story about America, we have to tell the good, the bad, and the indifferent. Americans want to paint this picture and feel that everything is so pristine, so lovely, but if you go back and you look at his history. 1619, now freed slaves, he had no money, he had no land, guess what he went back and did, he went right back to the same situation, but they called it sharecropping, what are we sharing is this 50/50, no, you work for me, and I give you a place to stay, and I get all the benefit of the crop.

Some people are so hell-bent, on this is how it is, this is how it's going to be. Forget the fact that you benefit from what your ancestors did, benefiting from being white in America. You are at third base, I'm at home, I'm swinging but I already got 2 strikes, to deny that, I don't know why you would. I mean it's ok, when people say, well look you have muscles and I could run fast, I have an advantage. OK, I'm not going to say I don't have an advantage I, understand that working on the farm helped me to be more advanced than kids my age or grade.

But, for you to deny, that you benefited from this. Why? because all of a sudden, you're not as smart, you're not as hard-working as you would like for people to believe. talk about blacks being lazy, how can you help build America, I never understood that lazy, savages. Everything, that you see in a lot of black America is a learned behavior. Well, they learned it from how you did, you split them up and how you killed them and how you didn't allow them to vote and what you did to the Native Americans, everything they learn, they learn from you, total.

STOP, WHITEWASHING AMERICAN HISTORY

Melanie Moore facebook.com

"Good evening board members, my name is Melanie Moore, and I am the parent of a third and 4th grader in District 2. I'm, grateful for the opportunity, to speak with you this evening. The issue I would like to address is the need for equitable education in all areas". Sometimes, the truth hurts, when we look back and see why we are where we are, and the things that occurred, it hurts, maybe to some? To, try and hide it, is a big mistake, not good. Because, everything done in the dark, will surely come to the light. But, for us to move forward, with a clean slate.

We, have to come clean or stay away from dirty and some have chosen the latter. If you are thinking, the ole south will rise again, nope. Nothing stays the same, we as a people are constantly evolving. Here, is a little scenario, "I, would like to share something personal. I struggle with depression; I have for many years. I have gone to counselors throughout the years and one of the first things they ask me is, tell me about your family of origin, tell me about your past, what happened to you in your past, that is causing the current trauma and pain that you're feeling"?

In the same way, our country, cannot begin to heal until we deal with the pain, trauma, and hurt from our past. We, must teach our children the truth about the past and then show them how to be the change we wish to see in the world. We can help them connect the dots, from the awful events of the past to the current issues that face our country, so, that real change can happen. As, a member of the white community, we have got to stop pushing the agenda that diversity and truth in education are all about indoctrination shaming or placing guilt at the feet of white people.

No one is asking you to get up and place your head on the chopping block for the wrongs of the past, people are simply asking for their stories to be heard and taught, as ours have been for generations. I, would not allow my children to wallow in anger, pain, and self-pity. I would do all I could to help them to be the very best versions of themselves, even if it hurts to point out some painful truths about their behavior. In, the same way we have got to be honest with ourselves and admit that systemic racism is real, that this country was created and prospered under the ideals of white supremacy, and that we are responsible for righting the wrongs of our forefathers.

We, did not create this mess, but we are the ones that have to clean it up, starting with honest equitable education practices now, that will teach our children the hard truths about our past so that they can create a better future I understand that change is hard but it's got to come. racism is alive and well in this country it's, seen in the groups of white men with torches chanting, you will not replace too. Too, this year the fact is, that in 2021 we still don't have a federal anti-lynching hate crime law in the United States

We should know better, and then we have to do better, which creates pride in all of us, for where we live. We, know the old saying, happy wife happy life. But, how can we as a people be happy, when we hold on to the past, how can we grow, how can we mature? If you spend your days with your foot on another man's neck? When will you mature, when will you be the best that you can be, probably never because your days are spent worrying about keeping your fellow man down?

AMERICA, THE GREAT DIVIDE

Rev. Lewis Farrakhan

Talk about the lie, those white people who have settled this country. They had a fatal flaw. Caucasians could recognize a man when they saw one. They knew he wasn't anything else but a man. But, since they were Christian, they had already decided, that they came here to establish a free country. The only way to justify the role this channel was playing in one's life. What' to say that he was not or if he wasn't? saying here at the heart of it is that there have been lies told about African people lies about our character, about our passions, all to justify this system of exploitation.

This system, this cruel barbaric system of slavery, is at the heart of the founding of this modern world, right, at the heart. How you have lied about Africans. what white Americans have done to Africans. This, is the key point, any real effort to expose the reality of what they have done, anything that comes to reveal the truth of what the nation has done to the native people, what it has done in Haiti and Cuba, and the Philippines. What, it has done in Hiroshima Nagasaki.

Anything, that reveals that America is not the shining city on the hill or the Redeemed nation or the example of democracy achieved. Anything, that attempts to reveal the reality is immediately dismissed. This heresy, that lie, is the architecture within which fundamental belief that white people, matter more than others and that's at the heart of this sedition, political arranged evaluation of Africans and evaluation of life that led to the distribution of advantage and disadvantage, that distorts their character.

 So, they can't even become the kinds of people their conception of democracy requires. The lie has been told too many times about Africans, that you're less beautiful, less intelligent if you run around scared intimidated, and fearful all the time and laughing, when it isn't funny and scratching when it doesn't itch, you're just going to wear a mask your whole life. The only thing that could break the back of fear, is love for one's self.

THE POLICE AND PRISON SYSTEM STARTED BY CATCHING SLAVES

Anointed hands facebook.com

People said, well, if we don't need black labor anymore, then what do we do with them? Well, we have to set up in the commercial system or at least incorporate black people into the commercial system, so that they make us money, without having to do the labor of working, picking cotton or picking sugar cane or whatever we already passed that make a more sophisticated plantation, where we can keep slaves. Well, let's criminalize pretty much every damn thing that we do, there, are over a million laws on the books.

Now, who needs a million Laws, unless you want to control the people's behavior. The police presence has always been in the black community because we are prisoners of war, that's number one. The original police were created as slave catchers, there was no need to police a white society, in early America. The police were always about guarding property that's what the police were about. Their job gets stretched out to moral responsibility and public safety, that kind of thing. Later on, in their development, the original concept of a police officer is to make sure your property stays with you.

 Hired by the rich, first to protect the richest property, 80% of prisons are found in republican districts. because you may have a town of let's say 20,000 people, let's say you have 20,000 prisoners in the prison system in your community when it's time to be taxed when it's time to get money from the government you have 40,000 people even though that 20,000 never get the money that is in prison, they're accounted for in your population.

 War on drugs was part of a grand republican party strategy, known as the southern strategy of using racially coded get tough appeals on issues of crime and welfare to appeal to poor and working-class whites, particularly in the South. Who are anxious about or resentful of many of the gains of African Americans in the civil rights movement and president Richard Nixon's former chief of staff Haldeman described the strategy this way and I believe I'm recalling the quote correctly "he said quote the whole problem is the blacks, the key is to devise a system that recognizes this will not appear to" end quote?

 people look at it as a civil rights violation, because it's criminal what they're doing to black people on a mass scale, criminalizing the image of black people and railroading them into a jail system really for profit that's slavery and that's a human rights issue and black needs to start treating that as a human rights issue we should not go to the courts here, because the courts here are in cahoots with the private organizations that are railroading all of these black men into the prison system. So, black people are going to do anything they need to take this fight to the world court to the world stage.

ENSLAVED AFRICANS IN 1619

The Final call

Slavery and democracy, you would think those concepts are opposed to the very cornerstone of our American democratic construct is the equal right to freedom and self-governance for all people. What, is the founders first began to shape the foundation of the Republic, they built slavery into it. On, this day in 1619 enslaved Africans, in the colony of Virginia were first recorded.

Those, men and women, were carried on Dutch ships to Jamestown. England's first permanent, colony in North America. The earliest form of democracy would also arrive in June of 1619, the first legislative assembly in the Western Hemisphere met in Jamestown. Laying, the foundation for the representative democracy we know today. This, assembly the House of burgesses was made up of Virginias, the 22 most powerful landlords. There is a disregard for an uprising of farmers, indentured servants, and formerly enslaved people.

The group Marches on Jamestown, nearly burning it to the ground. As, a result the leaders of Jamestown created laws to punish the most vulnerable of this group, the enslaved people from Africa. While, the first Africans in Jamestown were allowed to buy their freedom, that all changed very quickly. The first legal sanctioning, of lifelong slavery in the colonies, came in 1640 by 1662 Virginia legally recognized slavery as a lifelong hereditary condition.

By, 1705 slavery laws had been codified all of this to fuel America's economic growth. Slave, labor became essential, for the agriculture sector especially for tobacco and cotton according to Pulitzer Prize-winning author James MacPherson in 1860. Then nearly four million, African American slaves were worth some $3.5 billion, making them this large in the entire U S economy worth more than all manufacturing and railroads combined. Losing, all of that built on the backs of enslaved people was the original economic anxiety. So, today we reflect on slavery democracy, and the price of freedom that is for the culture.

136

RACISM IN AMERICA

Phil Vischer facebook.com/

We, need to talk about race, why are people protesting, why are people angry, slavery ended 150 years ago, the civil rights movement was 60 years ago, racial discrimination is illegal, and now we even had a black president. So, why are people still upset? We're, going to go through and show you these Americas, one is black, the other is white. Today, the average black household has 60% of the income of the average white household, but only 1/10th of the household wealth. Why, does that matter? Well, household wealth helps send kids to school, helps launch small businesses, stabilizes loss of income, and helps families survive catastrophic events, like divorce or unemployed.

What's amazing about this number, is that there are lots of extremely wealthy African Americans, movie stars, pop stars, 75% of the NBA, 70% of the NFL, Oprah, Tyler Perry, Ben Carson, Morgan Freeman, and there are a lot of extremely poor white families. Think, of Appalachia and other parts of rural America, but even when we factor all that in, the average African household still has only 1/10th the wealth of the average white household, how did that happen? Well, here we go. What, happened after we freed the slaves after the civil war ended?

 Nine, states enacted vagrancy laws, making it a crime to not have a job. The law was applied only to black men. In eight of those states, the black men, who had just been arrested for not having a job, to were hired out to plantation owners, with little or no pay going to the prisoners themselves. So, that's right, men who had been freed from the plantations found themselves right back on the plantations. Additionally, laws prohibited mischief and insulting gestures, which allowed more black men to be arrested creating a huge market for convict leasing. working conditions for these least convicts could be worse than slavery, because the plantation owner leasing the black prisoner, had no long-term interest in his well-being.

By, the turn of the 20th century, every state in the South had mandated racial segregation by law. Jim Crow laws, supported schools, churches, housing, jobs, restrooms, hotels, restaurants, hospitals, prisons, funeral homes, morgues, and cemeteries. White, politicians competed with each other, to be stricter and more specific on segregation, for example, a law prohibiting blacks and whites from playing chess together, and no interracial chess playing that might lead to lawn darts. In, 1896 the Supreme Court ruled "that these Jim Crow laws were perfectly legal because they quote, reflected customs and traditions and quote preserved public peace and good order," these laws stayed in place until 1954.

When, the idea of separate, but equal was struck down in the ruling known as Brown versus Board of Education? So, what happened next after brown? Well in 1956, the southern manifesto was signed by 101 out of 128 Congress members from the South, pledging to maintain Jim Crow by all means possible. Five, states passed nearly 50 new Jim Crow laws, and after 1954 private whites-only schools, dubbed segregation academies popped up all across the South, many of them Christian!

But now widespread civil rights protests combined with anti-war protests, that were occasionally becoming violent inspired the political rise of law-and-order rhetoric.

 Richard Nixon, became the first candidate to campaign specifically on a platform of law and order, in 1968, 81% of Americans, agreed that law and order had broken down in this country and the majority blamed communists and "Negros who start riots." Let's, go back to household wealth, the average African black household has $1/10^{th}$ the wealth of the average white household, why is that? because the number one source of intergenerational wealth, in America, is home ownership and from the 1930s to well into the 1960s, the federal government enacted policies to actively, encourage white families to own homes and discourage black families from doing the same.

In, 1934 the Federal Housing Administration, created a risk rating system to determine which neighborhoods, were safe investments for federally backed mortgages. Black, neighborhoods were deemed too risky, marked off on maps with red ink, in a practice now known as redlining. After World War two, a boom of new suburban housing was built, all over the country much of it restricted by deed to whites only. In, 1948 forty percent of new housing in Minneapolis, for example, had covenants prohibiting purchase by African Americans.

So, blacks couldn't live in white neighborhoods and couldn't get federally insured loans for black neighborhoods, until 1950. The Realtors code of ethics, specifically prohibited selling a house in a white neighborhood to a non-white family, you could lose your realtors license, if you help the black Purchase a home in a white neighborhood. In the 1930s, the FHA underwriting manual said quote "incompatible racial groups should not be permitted to live in the same communities, the FHA went on to recommend that highways would be a great way to separate black neighborhoods from white neighborhoods." The FHA funded, huge wide only suburban housing developments, leaving blacks behind in inner cities.

After World War two, the GI bill provided subsidized mortgages to help millions of men returning from war to buy their first home, while technically eligible, the GI bill the way it was administered, left 1,000,000 black veterans largely on the outside looking in. In New York and New Jersey, the GI bill insured more than 67,000 new mortgages, fewer than 100 of those went for homes purchased by nonwhites. In, 1947 there were 3200 mortgages in Mississippi guaranteed by the government for returning veterans of the 3200 only two went to black veterans, as a result, white families after the war, were able to build home equity growing wealth for retirement, inheritance, and college education for their kids. One, the historian has stated that there was no greater instrument for widening an already huge racial gap in post-war America than the GI bill.

And, then came the war on drugs, inner-city blacks were extremely vulnerable economically, the overwhelming majority of African Americans in 1970 lacked college degrees and had grown up in fully segregated schools. In the second half of the 20th century, factories and manufacturing jobs moved to the suburbs, black workers struggled to follow the jobs, and they couldn't live in many neighborhoods. And as late as 1970, only 28% of black fathers had access to a car. When, a white man in Cicero IL, just outside Chicago, sublet an apartment to a black family the white community rioted, setting fire to the apartment building and smashing windows, until the National Guard had to intervene.

Result of all of this, in 1970, 70% of African American men had good blue-collar jobs, by 1987 only 28% did. As unemployment skyrocketed in African American communities, so did drug use, and as drug use increased, so did crime a dynamic today, that we see playing out in white rural communities hit hard by unemployment and opioid addiction. Throughout, the 1970s, white America, became increasingly concerned by images of black violence shown on TV and in magazines. Drugs were the problem, and drug dealers and drug users were the enemies so we decided to treat the drug epidemic not as a health crisis but as a crisis of criminality and we militarized our response during the Reagan and Bush years.

From 1981 to 1991, How we invested money in anti-drug allocation completely changed the anti-drug budget, for the Department of Defense, which went from $33 million in 1981 to more than $1 billion in 1991. The Drug Enforcement agency's budget to fight criminality and drug use went from $86 million to more than a billion dollars. Then, we came to the 1980s which carried mandatory minimum sentences, much harsher for the distribution of crack cocaine, which was associated with blacks than powder cocaine which was associated with whites. Mandated evictions from public housing, for any tenant who permitted drug-related criminal activity to occur on or near premises.

That, eliminated many government benefits, including student loans for anyone convicted of a drug crime. The 1988 revision, said a five-year minimum sentence, for possessing any amount of crack cocaine, even if there was no intent to distribute, previously had been a one-year maximum sentence for possessing any amount of any drug, without the intent to distribute, it might seem like we're picking on Republicans. So, now the Democrats, during the Clinton presidency, the funding for public housing was cut by $17 billion, and at the same time, the funding for prisons increased by $19 billion. The number of Americans in prison for drug crime exploded. In, 1980 there were 41,000 Americans in prison for drug crimes most arrests for possession. In 2000, more than the entire 1980 prison population possession in 2005, 80% of the arrests were for possessing drugs not selling drugs in a bizarre twist.

We also militarized our police forces. Between 1997 and 1999 the Pentagon handled 3.4 million orders for military equipment from more than 11,000 police agencies including, 253 aircraft Blackhawk and Huey helicopters, 7800 M16 rifles, 181 grenade launchers for the police, 8000 bulletproof helmets, 1200 night vision goggles, we also changed policing tactics a no-knock entry is when a swat team literally breaks down your door or smashes in through the windows, like in the movie ET when the cops come flying in from every direction looking for ET. so back to Minneapolis in 1986 Minneapolis swat teams performed no-knock entries 35 times, 10 years later, in 1996 they performed no-knock entries 700 times that's two every day.

There were financial incentives, for arresting more drug users. Federal, grants to local police departments were tied to the number of drug arrests. Research, suggests the huge surge in arrests, from increased Drug Enforcement, was due more to budget incentives than to actual increases in drug use. So, what was the result? an explosion of our prison population. In, 25 years the US prison population went from 350,000 to over 2.3 million, the United States now has the highest rate of incarceration in the world. We, imprison a higher percentage of our African black population than South Africa ever did during apartheid.

Data shows that the increased prison population, was driven primarily by changes in sentencing policy, there was no visible connection between higher incarceration rates and higher violent crime rates. If you are a drug felon, you are barred from public housing, you are ineligible for food stamps, and you're forced, to check the box on employment applications, marking yourself as a convicted felon, shown to reduce the likelihood of getting a callback or job offer, by as much as 50%.

The negative impact of a criminal record for an African American job applicant is twice as large, as for a white applicant. In, 2006, one in 106 white men was behind bars, for black men it was one in 14, for black men between the age of 20 and 35, the age where families are built, it's one in nine. Overall, African Americans and white Americans use drugs at roughly the same rate, but the imprisonment rate of African Americans for drug charges is almost six times that of whites.

It may be true that there isn't explicit racism in our legal system anymore, but it doesn't mean justice is blind. A study, in Georgia, permitted imprisonment for a second drug offense, throughout the study this law was used against 1% of white second-time offenders and 16% of black second-time offenders as a result 98% of prisoners serving life sentences under this law were black, African American youth in the US make up 16% of all youth, but 28% of all juvenile arrests, 35% of youth set to adult court, instead of the juvenile court and 58% of youth admitted to adult state prison.

Study, blacks on the New Jersey Turnpike make up 15% of all drivers, but 42% of all stops by police and 73% of all arrests among all drivers stopped. White drivers were two times more likely than black drivers to be carrying drugs. Study, the Lucia County Florida 5% of drivers were black or Latino but 80% of drivers stopped were black or Latino. Study, in Oakland CA black drivers are twice as likely as white drivers to be stopped and three times more likely to be searched. In Minneapolis, Philando Castile had been pulled over 49 times in 13 years, mostly for minor infractions, the 49th time he was pulled over he was shot by the officer while sitting inside his car he'd been pulled over for a broken taillight.

Chuck Colson's organization, prison fellowship recently organized a manifesto silicle leaders asserting that our over-reliance on incarceration fails to make us safer or restore the people in communities who have been harmed unconscious, bias seeps into schools too as white teachers often assume black students are less intelligent than they are. A gifted student usually has to be recommended by a teacher, to move to a gifted track. When a teacher is black and equally gifted white and black students have comparable chances of being recommended. When the teacher is white, the black students' odds of being recommended are cut in half. Are white teachers racist? no, are they affected by bias? Yes, and it affects black students every day.

 So here are why, the average black household has 1/10th the wealth of the average white household, this didn't happen by accident it happened by the policy. We the majority culture told them where they could live and where they couldn't. Then we moved most of the jobs, which would create a predictable explosion of unemployment and poverty resulting in a predictable increase in drug use and crime.

 America created a problem; we criminalize the problem we built $19 billion in new jails and sold grenade launchers to the police as a result of a white boy born in America. today has a one in 23 chance of going to prison in his lifetime for a black boy it's one in four and that is why people are angry many people care deeply about these issues many have suggested solutions some of which have been tested with results ranging from moderate success to abject failure I'm not here to tell you what the right solutions are because I don't know I'm just here to ask you to do one thing it is the thing that begins every journey to a solution what am I asking you to do? Care for the ones that built this country, from their blood sweat, and tears.

WE ARE STILL HERE

When we talk about buck breaking, we have to understand that buck breaking is a show of power a show of dominance, so we can't talk about buck breaking without talking about power. When we look at the domination of African people by the dominant society, what we are in essence seeing is that this society wants to ensure that we are not able to meet out that thing that makes humans exist and that is creating families and procreating psychologically.

When, we're talking about the sexualizing of our people, primarily from the dominant society, but the system of white supremacy it had to be established in a very impinging way from the mental state all notion that 212masculinity is somehow toxic and detrimental to society, is nothing but an attempt to emasculate black male hood. it's an agenda, if you have two eyes in your head and you're able to see, you can see that it's an agenda to decrease our population. It's always been about destroying the black family the Family Foundation of the people; the heterosexual black male is the last on the pecking order here in America.

 If you are a heterosexual black man and you show up in court, how are you going to beat the case? when you show up to court when you show up to the job interview when you show up to wherever, you coming in here as a heterosexual black man, you have no power. When Mark Twain confessed, that we white people have to ground the manhood out of the negro, why ground the manhood out of the negro male? because it's the African male masculinity mostly, that exposes the fraud of the white male masculinity.

We, as the progenitors of culture the ones who are the fathers and mothers of civilizations, who taught all people. If anyone should have a problem with European males, it should be European females, because everything that European male has ever learned to do to us, he first practices on his own woman. we need resources and education we need resources and labor we need resources in politics we need resources and medical, and we need resources in so many things' millions embrace your LBGT side so these people have an agenda and it's up to us to understand what the agenda is.

MODERN-DAY CONFEDERATES:

Occupy Democrats facebook.com

"America is false to the past, false to the present, and solemnly binds herself to be false to the future" those were the words of Frederick Douglass former slave, turned national leader for the abolition of slavery. whose opinion President Abraham Lincoln said was the most important in the nation. A month before the end of the civil war, Lincoln called for the union to honor black Americans, with the right to vote and three days later he was shot and killed by the confederate terrorist, John Wilkes Booth and Lincoln had picked a southerner, Andrew Johnson as his vice president in the hopes of unifying a divided country.

When Johnson took over the presidency, he was supposed to oversee the prosecutions of 39 confederate leaders, responsible for the bloodiest war in U.S. history, that the South thought was a righteous rebellion to protect slavery. Judge, John C Underwood presided, over the case and he was furious, those confederate leaders with their hands dripping with the blood of our slaughtered innocent, and martyred president, were still at large. Judge underwood's court, issued a warning, that failure to convict would embolden future rebellions and more acts of treason.

He spoke to the jury directly and he said it's for you to teach them that who sow the wind must reap the whirlwind, that clemency and mercy to them would be cruelty and murder to the innocent and unborn. Confederate general, Robert E Lee, and the southern shadow president, Jefferson Davis faced capital punishment if they were to be found guilty. The charge was, being moved and seduced by the instigation of the devil, to subvert, disturb, move and incite insurrection rebellion, and war against the United States of America. But there were countless delays, president Johnson was protesting, against including black jurists, and one month before the end of his term Johnson just drops all the charges.

Robert E Lee and Jefferson Davis and 37 other confederate leaders, just walk away, in fact, the only

American found guilty of treason during the civil war was John Brown. An abolitionist, who fought to end slavery and for that brown was hanged for the crime of treason, against Virginia, and witnesses to his hanging were none other than general Robert E Lee and John Wilkes Booth. For general Lee and the Confederates, there'd be no convictions, and what happened next, was northern congressmen didn't want to seat Confederates sympathizers in Congress. They want a union military presence, in the southern states to maintain law and order and they want to pass protections for black America.

President Johnson vetoed those protections and fired one of his so-called radical cabinet members who agrees with them as a result, Johnson is the first president to be impeached, but he escapes conviction in the Senate and so reconstruction and reconciliation are compromised and crippled. Statues of Robert E Lee and Jefferson Davis are built to commemorate white supremacy and treason and myths around states' rights and southern pride, live on as a transparent cover for the shame of an ideology of extreme brutality and delusional supremacy and that culture of the confederacy rises again and again. antidemocratic anti-science anti-black, anti-brown, anti-immigrant, and anything that isn't their clan.

Century after century, so-called white moderates, find unscrupulous reasons to accommodate, these white supremacists for their self-interest, for their lack of courage. Black America, Native America, and everyone else is dammed. So, now we see today, rising from the boneyards of America's unatoned sins, a terrorist sympathizer who signaled approval for political assassinations, who disparages Jews and Muslims who publicly harass child survivors of school shootings. Which claims are just conspiracies to take away our guns, who Republicans elected into our Congress and republican leadership?

These people are not only uninterested in unity, they openly embrace political violence. This is not white privilege, it's our recurring white nightmare haunting century after century, with their so-called suicidal fantasy that nobody belongs here but them. 147 Congress members committed treason when they voted to overthrow our democracy. 147 Congress members, now claim with forked tongues to have only represented the hordes that welcomed their lies. No, those 147 traitors who made every effort to subvert, stir, move and incite insurrection and rebellion against our country must be expelled from public office tried and convicted in a court of law.

Their sponsors, enablers, and promoters must all face boycotts and cancellations and be hauled into court on charges of sedition for the millions of descendants of African slaves and the survivors of Native American, and Holocaust for every citizen of our migrant nation who believes in equality for all people. It is for you to teach them, that those who sow the wind must reap the whirlwind that clemency and mercy to them would be cruelty and murder to the innocent and unborn in the words of "Frederick Douglass if this war is to be forgotten, I ask in the name of all things sacred. what shall men remember, we must never forget that victory to the rebellion meant death to the Republic".

KNOWLEDGE OF AFRICA WAS NEVER MEANT, FOR THE WORLD TO KNOW.

Good Vibes Home.facebook.com

If you read what the Greeks said, not what we think, but if you read what the Greeks said. They said they got everything from Egypt, they got all their knowledge from Egypt. Pythagoras, spent 15 years in Egypt and what did he have to do? He probably had to spend five years convincing them, that he was worthy to get the knowledge that they had. Remember, knowledge was power, knowledge was sacred. No, it was not something you just didn't publish in the newspapers, knowledge was guarded very closely because it was of tremendous value. You wouldn't give it to anybody, they would give it to somebody, who was willing to shave his head and be a penitent for five years. Then they might start to tell him things.

The Greeks did this, Pythagoras did this, other Greeks did this and they said that they got all their knowledge from the Egyptians. Now, when did we come up with the idea that the Greeks created everything from scratch? Well, believe it or not, it happened in the 18th and 19th centuries and it's an unfortunate fact of life, that romanticism, which has many great things about it also has a dark side. Which, has to do with racism and then the 18th and 19th centuries. It was decided, that it was just not appropriate for all this knowledge to come from an African country. Where? would that knowledge if it survived to the time of the Roman Empire, where would it have been kept in Alexandria and the museum the library at Alexandria, and what happened to the library? it was burned.

WHAT WAS DONE IN THE DARK, WILL COME TO LIGHT

Amber Ruffin facebook.com

More than 1000 black residents of Forsyth County Georgia, were forced from their homes. Their homes, land, and all they had worked so hard for, were taken away because of the color of their skin. They owned the land, and paid taxes on it, but for them as owners, was deleted from court records, but there are records of the land being sold in parcels by white men. And, the blacks were forced off their land into the night, like cattle being herded. I don't know, why people think that at no point they don't have to reconcile with our past to have peace in the future, even to come to Christ, we have to reconcile with our past.

What makes America so different? and to say this country was built on Christianity, oops you could have fooled me. This is how one such county in Georgia is now facing its racist past. This is why, some don't want critical race theory taught in schools, because it paints a vivid picture of the atrocities committed by our founding fathers, they were monsters. One such town has to reckon with its past. In, a narrow patch of forest, between rows of half-million-dollar homes, even looking straight down from the air, nothing raises the mystery of what lies beneath! Second, stones are all that's left of the old black Baptist Church at Stony Point.

If you were able and looking closely at the headstones, they all predate 1912, why do they all end before 1912? this is not evidence of promises broken, but loved ones kept away. Because the men women and children buried here were the only black residents of Forsyth County Georgia. For nearly all of the 20th century, negro people had to leave their homes and land. Because there was knocking on the door and they were told to get out. She heard all those stories directly from her mother, Willie Mae Bagley.

Just a 2-year-old, back in 1912 when the night riders came, they always come at night. my mother, different (Willie Mae) said, men, love the dark because their deeds are evil. The night riders would come, to their home and so many others, who were black in Forsyth County. Can you imagine the fear, that they would have felt, William and Ida Bagley? paying taxes on 60 acres, they owned in 1912 to find out, no record of any sale in the County Courthouse, except those of white men later selling parcels of the Bagley's land, to one another. The 1910 census showed the Bagley's among 1098 black residents of the county a tenth of the total population by 1920 nearly every last one of them was gone.

 long stretches where decade after decade the black population of Forsyth County Georgia was 0. Historical photos show only white faces after 1912 So what happened that year? thousands turned out to celebrate the public hanging of two black teenagers convicted in a single day of raping and murdering a white girl, named Meg Crow. If you believe that, you should watch the movie Rosewood massacre. The other black suspect had already been lynched, right here on the Cumming courthouse square.

The lynching of Rob Edwards involved a very large crowd, gathered outside the jail, dragging him out of the jail, beating him with crowbars, and dragging his body around town behind a wagon. And, then eventually, his corpse is hoisted on a Telegraph pole, and everyone in the crowd, takes turns shooting into his body, how sick is that? I would be ashamed also. just across from the spot where Rob Edwards was lynched, lady justice faces history, wearing her blindfold.

but soil from the square has been collected in a jar, and the name Rob Edwards will soon join the lynching memorial at the equal justice initiative. Some people are so ashamed, of how our forefather's acted they don't want their children to know the truth. But the sad part is, how can you go to any place without a starting point? No matter how some try to hide the past, our children are a lot smarter than we were, they will find the truth. The sad part is, we send them to school to learn and then we lie to them!!!!

AFTER SLAVERY, WE WERE NOT TOO SURVIVE

Amber Ruffin facebook.com

Over the past couple of years, more Americans have become familiar with the story of the Tulsa race massacre, where a white mob burned a vibrant black community to the ground. Which is crazy, even crazier dozens of other black towns have been erased off the American map, not by burning them down, but by hiding them underwater. Lake Lanier, it's a lake in Forsyth County Georgia, where people go swimming and boating and fishing and do a bunch of other laky things, but before it was lake Lanier it was a town called Oscar Ville Georgia. Now, Oscar Ville was a thriving predominantly black community with a church, a school, and dozens of homes until the year 1912.

When a very bad thing happened. In, 1912 two black teenagers were accused of rape, they were tried, convicted, and sentenced to death in a single day, and after the teens were executed, the white mob ran off or killed all the black people in the surrounding area and they did that until the entire black community of Oscar Ville disappeared. The county went from having over 1000 black residents in 1912 to 0 in 1920 that story is so sad. After the blacks in the community had been run off, the white people of Forsyth County said you know what we could use is a big old lake, so they made one right where the town of Oscar Ville had just been they flooded the area and covered up the entire town with water.

The town is still under the water, the homes, churches, and schools they're still down there and now people go boating on top of them. You might be thinking, what a weird isolated incident? This story is both crazy and common, ever heard of Calleja Alabama it was once a thriving black community with a black college, the first black railroad, and hundreds of family homes. Today it's lake Martin.

If, you think this kind of thing only happens in the south, let me introduce you to a place called Central Park. Central Park used to have a black community which was called York hill, but the city of New York destroyed York Hill to build a reservoir. when the residents of York hill were kicked out of their homes, they fled to another black community nearby called Seneca Village and then a few years later New York destroyed Seneca Village too so that they could build Central Park on top of it. The craziest part of this story is that many people who live and work here never knew the government disappeared two black communities and until recently I didn't know about any of it you know why because it worked.

They tried to erase black communities and they came way too close. But now people are doing the research, so we are finally learning about places like Henry and McKee Island, which is under Lake Guntersville in Alabama, and Vanport Oregon which is now located under Delta Park. Now, all of these towns are currently literally underwater.

There are over 100 drowned American towns, just to name a few Kenneth, Baird, Elmore and Morley California, Cibola, Sa Pinero, and Dillon Colorado, Jerusalem Connecticut, Old Fairfield Indiana, Warren Maryland, Dana, Enfield, Greenwich Massachusetts,

Prentiss Mississippi, Brown's Station, and Old Never sink New York and many were destroyed in the name of something called development induced displacement that's when people have to leave their homes so the government can develop things like dams or parks or lakes this happens to both white and black people.

But historically when it happens, black people and other people of color are under-compensated for their property or not compensated at all. The theory is that the short-term bad effects are worth the long-term benefits for the community. But, it's not fair if the long-term gain is mostly for white people. Now, luckily there's a solution, it's a very complicated system it involves a series of all. Who? am I kidding just cut a check, that's it, if you're going to kick black people out of their homes, make sure they have the money to stay on their feet, cut a check and yes you can pay their descendants too because generational wealth is one of the many things that is destroyed.

when you put black communities underwater, so cut a check, these drowned towns are part of black American history. They know all too well it's ugly and it's gross. They know all of it, and the more we find out, the harder it is to love this place, that would do those things to so many people, and if you're feeling this way, which I often do. You can try loving what this country could become instead. Our history may be full of pain but our future has limitless possibilities.

SYSTEMIC RACISM, WHAT'S THAT??

JP Sears facebook.com

Some people think, there's a problem with systemic racism in our country and there has been for a long time. Some don't see it. For an example of how some don't see it. They think back, I was raised in a predominantly white town in Ohio. When I was a kid, we would go to church on Sundays, I'd walk in and see the all-white congregation, a friend of the church, a white pastor, and above him a picture of white Jesus, with beautiful blue eyes. Was Jesus the only white guy in the Middle East 2000 years ago, before jet travel was a thing. Yes, or so I thought, but come to find out probably not but there's a perfectly good explanation for this.

Jesus had Brown skin and they didn't like that, does that make sense by painting him white. All of the white people were racially rejecting our Lord and savior based on the color of his skin. They couldn't accept him, so they are doing the opposite of blackface, they white face Jesus but once they did that then we could accept him as our Lord and savior because now he had white skin like them. I'm like what the naysayers think, we don't call that racism, we call that religion.

So, you can't question it or get angry let me bring it down like this, Jesus our Lord and savior is perfect in all ways and is made in the image of God, that wasn't good enough for them you had brown skin so there's nothing to work with, but once the white people fixed him by painting him white, then he was God-like, then he was fit to be their Lord and savior. finally, it's just like when someone is not fit to be your driver because they're drunk but once they sober up then they can be a good driver so they are Jesus' skin color.

 it's like if you racially reject your Lord and savior because of the color of his skin then you probably really need his teachings, but you're not going to accept his teachings until you change the color of his skin, then once you do that you can accept his teachings and then you can pretend that you live his teachings, while you continue rejecting the actual person that the teachings came from because of the color of his skin and that's not racism because we never acknowledge that's what we were doing.

you know, when my grandkids grows-up they will want to know what it was like growing up in the 1980s and 90s? then they will ask who was my childhood hero, and I will tell him Michael Jordan one day years from now I just imagined how joyful it would be to share with my grandkids about my childhood hero. How I admired him, how he inspired me. Then, I'll look up at my wall and show them a poster of a white Michael Jordan. So, they can understand how great he was just as they did with Jesus. So yeah, I don't see any systemic racism happening. It's time, to make a change, and stand for equality.

EVERYTHING HAS A SEASON, EXCEPT PEOPLE OF AFRICAN DESCENT

David Haywood

Sometime a few years back, I told my daughter that I was going to purchase myself a mask of an animal face. She asked me, why was I going to do that? I told her that every animal has a season, but Africans are always in season. Just look what happen to Michael Vick, not saying what he did was right, but because of his skin color, they ended his career. A dog's life has more value than a person of African descent. This is nothing new, this goes way back. Look at the number of African men, that have died at the hands of those who should serve and protect.

Some of you, are too young to remember Emmett Till. A young African male's life was snuffed out at a young age. Someone has to step up and say enough is enough, I know it can be done. I am reminded of school integration, former president Lynden B. Johnson, informed the south that you will integrate. What we have today, is school integration because someone stepped up and said enough is enough, so, don't tell me it can't be done. I can't, wrap my mind around such hatred, one man for another.

If America was founded on Christianity, where is love? Did we lose it in all the progress? When one of us dies at the hand of the police, they are saying Africans don't matter. I am reminded, of the children of Israel and Egypt. Not saying that Africans are the children of Israel or the Caucasians are the Egyptians, nothing stays the same.

The pharaoh of Egypt, instructed the midwives to kill all the boy babies, in the south, African women went to the doctor for an issue, he would give them a hysterectomy, this was also in part to stop the reproduction of the African. Then pharaoh ordered, to throw the babies in the Nile River, which didn't work either, just as now-a-day they just shoot us down in the streets, trying to stop the normal process.

What makes one man commit such vile acts against another man, that is not of God, because God is LOVE, where is yours? Everyone knows our worth but us because everything was stolen or wiped from our memory. Now that we are coming into our own, I guess, that is what makes them afraid. Mr. Cobb tried to deny his black history and that he is white. Life began around the fertile crescent of the Nile River which is in Africa and everything in the region is dark shinned. The African is not shown as being a hero, loving, or smart with none of those characteristics, so, let's just eliminate the African from the pages of history, pharaoh also tried that as well.

STOP, INJECTING YOUR ANGER AND RAGE, INTO ME

David Haywood

Just want to give you a little something to think about, we've all heard that phrase, stop being the angry black man or black woman. But how can we, when the powers that be, won't let us? I saw just the other day, a woman who said I'm not an angry black woman. We, often fight that tag, well I'm not going to fight it anymore. Black folk has a reason, decades of racism and unfair treatment, unfulfilled dreams, and rule changes, right in the middle of the game, when we start winning.

Yep, we're angry and with good damn reason underpaid undervalued, underrepresented. Remember the NFL Rooney rule put in place to give us more black coaches more than some 20 years ago, still, a huge problem, and yet they continue to tell us to stop being so angry. No, I say I'm angry, you continue to kill me, cheat me and try to tell me otherwise. Yes, we are angry, maybe not angry enough? Certainly, here lately, I've seen anger from others, for far less reason, including just simply putting a face mask on and no apologies.

I say, I am an angry black man, but not without reason and not so angry that I let it sidetrack me or let the rage take me over for very long, to stop me in my tracks. And at times, well I do have to bring it back, don't look for our ability to control that anger as we have or that rage to last forever you see angry people do angry things so rather than telling black folks to stop being so angry, I say we need to stop apologizing saying we're not if you want us to stop being angry, I say stop giving a **** to be angry about just my thought, from an angry black man.

AND THE SALE'S NEVER STOP, EVEN TO THIS DAY

Henry Louis Gates, Jr.

Nearly half a million Africans survived the first middle passage, eventually arriving in the United States. But, a second middle passage inside our country was over twice as large in scale. The domestic slave trade fueled the nation's booming cotton economy and, in the process, shattered black families. After Eli Whitney, invented the cotton gin in 1793.

Cotton exploded as a cash crop. You have the technological innovation; the cotton gin makes it quicker, and easier to separate the seeds from the cotton bowl itself and you also have the Louisiana purchase and the seizing of indigenous Native American land as a result of that you have this new land in the west as a result demand for cotton and demand for labor. Slave owners from states in the upper South sold their slaves to traders who then transported them to the cotton-producing states in the deeper South and further to the West this came to be known as the second middle passage and its effects on the African American community would be devastating.

 They were forcibly sold, separated from families, husbands from their wives, and parents from children's siblings from one another forced to make these trips chained and bound together and clearing the way for the settlement of white Americans. About a million slaves move between these older States and the newer states in the South over three decades in the 19th century. So, there's this massive slave trade domestically that attend the opening of the cotton territory and the rise of the cotton kingdom in the South

Countless families became the victims of the largest forced migration in our country's history, but there was huge profit, we offer black bodies once they arrived at their destination families that have made the journey together often were ripped apart as the slave trade in Africa. the domestic slave trade scrambles any kind of community that black people had come to know and it leads to this new round of massive alienation and forced them to start all over again this horrendous dislocation lasted until the civil war began but the consequences of the second middle passage devastated generations of black families.

I'M COMING UP

Let's look at America, we went to Africa and brought back black slaves. We never intended them to be anything other than a slave. but they began to grow in numbers and power and eventually they fought their way to some freedom. So, we became even crueler to keep our black Americans down we lynched them, but yet they rose.

So, then we used the welfare system, the criminal justice system to keep them down to contain them, to destroy them, but yet they rose and their rising, then we build prisons and jails to hold them yet they rose and so now we are doing exactly what the pharaoh did, at the end sending out a decree killer them. So, until we admit, that when we wrote this constitution that all men are created equal that we never intended to include our black brothers and sisters.

Our nation may end up facing exactly what the Egyptians face when they refused to let God's people go. So, I'm going to say this to my white fellow Americans the bloodshed that's on its way, it's not from the hands of our fellow black Americans but from our hands. We are the ones, that are refusing to let God's people go, we are the ones that are refusing to acknowledge that, we do not value our black brothers and sisters as equal individuals or equal Americans as a white men and to my black brothers and sisters the racial issues as I've said have been there from the very foundation.

But why do we see it more? Because there is a shifting, see us white men have been at the head since the foundation, but we have had a black president and you know we've done everything in our power to keep him from really changing things. Now, we have another minority rising to the top, a white female, what does that say to those of us who are white men, who have been at the head and are now starting to see and fear that we are going to become the tail and we know what we've done to you and so now we're fearful that you're going to do to us but we have done to you.

I've lived in a black community for 23 years, and I've never been treated the way this country has treated its blacks, so I call out my white Americans to say we better heed repent acknowledge and change because if we don't, I just want to again say this, the bloodshed that we will experience is on our hands not the hands of our fellow black Americans.

THE PLANTATION MENTALITY, IS TO KEEP THEM BROKE

Dr. Umar Johnson

The issue with cops is a black and white thing, No question about it, and police abuse of power. when slavery ended in 1865, there were no national incarceration systems most states didn't even have a fully functioning prison system until 1865. That's when they gave you the first statewide prison systems. We got 4,000,000 Africans, just of slavery, they don't have jobs, they were not going to give them any.

So, that means they got to do what to eat, either Rob or steal. so, they create vagrancy laws, if I catch you stealing anything, guess what I'm going to put you on a chain gang and you're going to be on the chain gang for 10 years, for stealing whatever. If you did not have a job, you could go to jail for not having a job, you could go for being homeless, they make simple petty offenses major felonies. So, from the beginning of so-called emancipation, the prison system existed for one reason, to remove the African male from society.

The jail is a slave ship that sits on land instead of water, but here's the point I need y'all to understand, the reason we're struggling so much as the people. it's because we're not giving systematic access to wealth, let me give an example Chinese, Arab, East Indian they come to America, they can walk into any bank and get a loan, not all of them but many of them, some of them don't even have to get a bank loan.

Just to make the point, they show up in America with a long line of credit from their native country, they come into the ghetto open up 10 stores, 5 supermarkets, and 3 hotels black folks still struggling then people look at us and say you know why you're struggling because you're lazy the Chinese guy over here been here five years the East Indian been here 10 years, we've been here eight years he got five gas stations, what's your excuse?

let me tell you what's my excuses, we are systematically denied access to wealth do you understand so we can't build that hospital they built we can open up 10 supermarkets I can't get ten gas stations in three weeks because you're going to routinely deny me access to wealth, you'll give me a small business loan and here's the kicker, you will give me a student loan, a car loan for the car, they will give you a loan for your house, so you can get a mortgage loan.

Wait, a minute now the education is going to cost me 100 grand, the car is going to be about 70 grand, the house is going to be a quarter of a million why do you approve that but you don't approve the business loan which is probably for half the amount. Because, if I finance your empowerment that disrupts my system of extermination and genocide, you cannot kill people who you are financially empowering. so we are kept without access to wealth, that's why the hood is full of mom-and-pop stores, that's why the hood is full of struggling businesses because America has a policy, you do not empower black people for their benefit. any other minority yes, why because if they get out of hand, they could be sent home. The black man, cannot be sent home, slavery is older than

America, America was born on July 4^{th,} 1776, and slavery in the colonies began on August the 20th 1619

AMERICA! YOU MUST BE BORN AGAIN

Dr. Martin L. King Jr.

Now, I understand, when Martin Luther King said "America you must be born again." When America was formed, this was to be a new nation, old things passed away, and all things become new. And so it was, for a while, greed set in, then we became like where we came from, England. In the bible, if you look in Revelation: the second chapter, God said, I have something against you, that you have left you, first love! What was America's, first love? To create a place, where God could be served, with truth and honesty, love and brotherhood.

Someone said to me, that to see a problem and have no solution is counterproductive. There are ten commandments, if we cover, the first two, we pretty much have the other eight covered. Because, of so much deception, greed, dishonesty, sexual immorality, hatred of one for another, and most of all, we put God on the back burner, that is why the world was destroyed the first time with water and why there is so much trouble in the world today.

Then, we ask God to bless these United States, he already has! But the question is, when will these United States, bless God? Out, of the two most important things, God asked us to do are, love the Lord your God with all your heart, soul, and mind, then love your neighbor as yourself and we refuse to do. Because kindness is contagious, and it would spread like a wildfire.

Instead of loving our neighbor, we enslaved him, even until this day, then we ask God to bless us. God, has blessed America with amble waves of grain, modern medicine, modern technology, sending rockets to the moon, submarines, large ships, food, clothes, automobiles, houses, not caves and we can go from coast to coast in a matter of hours, all he asked, love me and love thy neighbor.

Sometimes a man wants to compare himself to or with God. I wouldn't like to be reminded as though we lived in

Sodom or Gomorrah because of its wickedness. It's easy to be born again, start loving God and treat people the way you want to be treated. Turn from our wicked ways and back to our first love, which was God, our neighbor, and country, and be transformed by the renewing of our mind.

MY HISTORY, IT'S STILL MINE

The good question now black people's skin contains carbon, carbon 12 is composed of 6 protons, 6 neutrons, and, 6 electrons which is the structure for melanin. Melanin comes from the sun, that's why people get darker in the sun because they absorb this melanin. right now, our DNA is locked, we only use 20 out of 64 amino acids, because the hotter that sun gets and the more, we are in it, it's unlocking our DNA.

See, in ancient times the Egyptians were in tune naturally with unlocked DNA, we were connected to the source of God, they knew how to live naturally and didn't need a book to be told how to live, because the Gods, had their pineal gland open. you see the cobras atop their head dress that symbolizes their kundalini energy rising and striking their pineal gland. So, the pharaoh with the pineal gland open was worshipped as a God.

Egyptians understood the power of the sun. Ra, the sun god of Egypt was always depicted with a picture of the sun atop his head. But they took away our true history and gave you all this story, you ever noticed how the picture of Jesus always had a halo of the sun about his head? they took the sun god and reversed him into the son of God.

Pharaohs were black, but then they whitewashed everything and when I say everything, I mean everything. just think about how black history doesn't go any further than slavery, nobody ever asked what we were doing before slavery because they don't want black people to know the truth about their history. Now, in case you don't know, we invented almost everything. Because we were slaves, we own nothing. The white male either bought or stole it from us, know they are putting our inventions up in museums and we even built the pyramids, and we were much larger humans.

Now, look, who's mostly in jail, who's mostly in gangs, who are mostly getting shot by police, who's mostly looked down on by this country? Black people, you think all this is happening only because our skin color is different, NO. Before slavery, white people knew how powerful we were but they enslaved us and now we're in their country, where they're on top and we're looked down upon, now people think of black people as thugs, especially the black males.

But how we fall from kings and gods, they programmed us to be that way. Why, do they promote rap music about killing and taking drugs, actually think about that? Rap music is the most promoted music. Every, ethnic group of people knows now their bloodline except Africans, you are not to know anything of your former self. That was part of the Willie lynch letters, that we knew nothing of our homeland or our culture, other than being a slave. But, because we are constantly being pushed down, and rising, the rest more to us than just a slave?

Take, all the African females, you were Queens as well, so what they give you in the place of a Queen, Nicki Minaj. We have been so programmed to be eye-appealing to their society. The reason why I say, we are so programmed to the point, where even if one black person woke up, he won't speak out or try to talk to his friends because he's scared of looking lame, real is not lame.

AFRICANS, NEEDED DARK SKIN

African Rise TV

Did you know, that those white people used to worship black deities? Negroes, were first worshipped in Greece and Rome. White, masses bowed down to black deities. The rights of Apollo were founded by Delphos and his Negro mother Malians, and the worship of black ISIS and Horus, which was popular in Rome and the Roman colonies as far north as Britain, was actually in ancient Rome. It, was common, for the Romans to make fun of their gods, but to worship and respect Horus and ISIS.

The worship of black ISIS and Horus existed as far north as Britain, but eventually, this evolved into the worship of the Black Madonna and the black Christ. Christian whites, also bowed down to the negroes as was said deified in early Greece, they appeared as gods in Greek mythology. The chief title of Zeus, the greatest of the Greek gods was aethiops, which means black. The, earliest of gods and messiahs on all continents were black, we have found the black complexion or related it whenever we have approached the origin of nations.

The alma mater of the goddess, the founder of the oracles, or the first idols were always black. The faces on the pyramids chipped the noses away, so it would be less apparent they were black. The oracles, that and the Apollo at Delphi, were founded by the black doves, oris and his bowl gods and goddesses of Greece were black at least it wasn't the case with Jupiter, Bacchus, Hercules, and Apollo. I'm on the goddess Venus, ISIS, Juno, Matisse, Searcy, and Sybil were black and the first God Zeus, Apollo, ISIS, Buddha, and Horhey were all black.

In the bible, in the accent days, God was described as having hair like pure wool the earliest deities were woolly-haired negroes. Their peppercorn hair was a sign of divinity, did you know that the Pope's private Chapel has a black Jesus in it. In, early Christian art, Jesus is almost invariably represented as black-skinned, the Hebrews were dark-skinned people. Jesus' feet were described as like burnt brass, in revelation. His hair was like wool also in revelation. my skin is black, Job.

They are black, Jeremiah. Looking out upon me, because
I am black Solomon, Joseph the Jewish historian wrote
that Christ was a man of simple appearance, mature age
dark-skinned with little hair and the earliest statues of the
Virgin Mary they're also black, everything was stolen
from Egypt.

RACISM, IS WHITE CULTURE

Sifiso MB TIKTOK

White culture is based on racism, it was a narrative created by colonizers like my Portuguese ancestors, to justify what they were doing to other people on the continent of Africa and even here in North America and the narrative was, that we, white people were better than all of the races and they did so through Christianity. They took the Bible and different scripture verses and twisted it around to fit the narrative of colonialism and white supremacy and also the patriarchy, the patriarchy is the white man in power.

White supremacy is a white man in power, colonialism is a white man in power, and Christianity for the most part nowadays is a white man in power. There are historical references in proof, where the Catholic Church said to enslave an African was to save their soul. The kidnapped and enslaved Africans, that were here in North America, were preached different scripture verses, that were actually in the Bible and that's why they weren't allowed to read because if they could read then they could see that these scripture verses were incorrect and they couldn't be controlled anymore by this white God and white people.

We didn't identify as white until colonialism. We were identified as Portuguese or Latvian or German or Italian or French, but then colonialism came around, and then all of a sudden, we became white and we were superior because we were the chosen race by God and the scripture verses proved it. We had to go into other people's lands and preach the gospel when it was all a ruse. It, was all an excuse, to go in and rape and pillage the land and the people and the cultures. So, when I say, that white culture is based on racism.

Christianity, was the Trojan horse of white supremacy and colonialism and western Christianity as we know it today, is still based on superiority. all Christians think that they're better than everybody else. I grew up in it, I'm very familiar with the culture and its part of the problem. There's a reason, why most of the trump supporters are Christians, realize that the conditioning of colonialism and Christianity and the patriarchy, is so deeply embedded within them and their identity, that they don't even see that true Christianity is based on white superiority in white culture, which is all based in racism.

WHITE AMERICA, LOVED WELFARE

The Breakdown facebook.com/

White America used to be very much in favor of welfare, especially when they were the only ones who benefited from it. So, we think about food allowances and cash allowances, which were originally put into place in the 1935 Social Security act. It was called, aid to families with dependent children. Then, the Social Security act deliberately excluded certain classes of people, from being able to get benefits, and among those it excluded nonwhites, by adding the clause domestic servants and agricultural workers could not get benefits. It landed a clause, where the states could determine if people in those positions, deserve those benefits or not.

Welfare is a really interesting subject because, on the one hand, we're familiar with the messaging to tear it down, but on the other, we know that programs such as Medicaid and Medicare, remains to be the most popular program. Social Security that the federal government has ever put forward. In fact, in 1935, the Social Security act put forth these programs in response to the economic fallout of the Great Depression. But, of course, at the time those benefits were only for white Americans primarily.

So, and in fact, the southern Dixiecrats said that they'd rather their people starve, instead of letting African Americans get any of these benefits. That type of messaging started to change the benefits of welfare programs. When the Civil Rights Act was passed, because then other people could have access to it, and now all of a sudden, they're getting our money we're paying for the others. But, the 1960s Civil Rights Act changed that and made these benefits available to everyone, and suddenly the messaging changed.

Starting in the 1970s, we start seeing oh we're building a nation of entitlement, a nation of people who think that they deserve things and this is a complete flip flop from earlier messaging. This is why, when we changed it in the 90s and of course, after the Civil Rights Act the tone and messaging on welfare began to change especially when we came into the Ronald Reagan administration. welfare Queens and how those types of things started to push in the messaging to then take down social programs. because now it's a waste of money, now it's fiscal irresponsibility, now, of course, we're paying for blacks and immigrants.

That's, why that messaging is transferred into things like universal healthcare, free education we give to people, it's going to make them weak, it's going to make them not want to work, it's going to make them want to sit at home and live off the government, when in reality, again these welfare programs are created, originally and still to this day. So, just help people get ahead, because when you give people a leg up when you help people get ahead just a little bit, typically most adults, are going to be responsible enough to do things like go to work.

I can remember living in Memphis, Tenn. In the '60s. The caseworker would come to my mother's house and they would, and did look under the bed and in her closet. The two things, they better not find, were a television or a man in her home. My mother did house cleaning and cooking for whites. She was paid $3.50 a day. In actuality, no one paid, social security or income tax. The same system, that was used by my mother, was used for her children as well.

Growing up, there were no fast foods or stores that teens could work in, that I remember. So, we went to the cotton field, to chop or pick cotton. What were our summer jobs, and who benefited from the system? Not us, for sure. All that, chopping and picking cotton, no one, had to pay social security or income tax for our labor, then they say, we were lazy.

Because people want to live a life of purpose. People, want to have an existence that means something. people don't want to just sit around on the couch and that's how the messaging has been flipped. If you're receiving welfare, if you're not white, then you're just lazy. But, if you're white, it's because he just needs some help.

The way institutional racism has kept itself alive is by keeping resources and access to benefits segregated at all costs. Whether that be from the very beginning of slavery. segregating things, like redlining, so when that started illegally face out, now just zoning laws, in general, make it so that if you're not white and wealthy, it's pretty much impossible to live in areas where everybody wants to be or at least if you're not wealthy, but still typically overwhelmingly is within the white community

So, that's how those things are still set up, we see how the prison industrial complex works. We see, that the majority of people whites and blacks, and Latinos do and sell drugs at pretty much the same rate. So, because of who does coke and who does crack primarily, we see the ways that these things work, but fortunately, for us, as technology continues to progress, as millennials move into positions of leadership, we have the opportunity to make societal welfare more popular because at the end of the day we know that we're not making people lazy.

we are just making society fairer and more equitable and making us more compatible on the world stage. Things like that, we're moving barriers to benefits and opportunities so that people who have talent can potentially participate in innovation, God gave them to the world stage.

SLAVE PTSD

Dr. Joy DeGruy

Slave, the syndrome is an explanatory theory, that looks at multi-generational trauma, and how it affects us, African Americans in the long run. One of the things, that's difficult for people is their first response is, oh my God that happened so long ago, then if that's the case, why doesn't it ever stop? We're talking about people being captured, shipped, sold, beaten, raped, and experimented on, and then, you have to ask the question, why, are we, the way we are?

The trauma continues yes, so 300 years of trauma. No help after slavery, when we were freed, from the Government who said, that we were citizens, just more trauma. If it's a sustained trauma, then the impact of that is also sustained. When we look at multi-generational trauma, we're looking at natural disasters, and experiences of war and we know that this residual mental-emotional traumatic impact and what happened, looking at the African American experience starting with slavery as a real clear long-enduring trauma, so we see that they were a clear connection between that survival behavior and contemporary living the African American experience.

As we, started to see common behaviors, that we took for granted as well as cultural, there are adaptive behaviors and survival behaviors well, what are they? let's say, you have a black mother and a white mother, in the parent-teacher conference, the black mother leans over to the white mother and says, I just wanted to mention to you that I notice, that your son is doing quite well, the white mother's response thank you, she began to go on and on about the science fairs, his uncles and astronaut, she just realizes the black mother-son is excelling as well, she says wait a minute, your son is the one that's coming along, then the black mother response, no he just works my nerves.

Now, when working with African American people, there's a secret, because everybody black knows, that even though the black mother is proud, she dares not let those words come from her lips, Oh my God, she's proud.

Roll that scene back, the white slave owner comes through and says wow that boy is coming along, what is she going to say? No, he's not, he's stupid, he's shiftless, he can't work because I don't want you to sell him? so, they denigrate them to protect them which is called appropriate adaptation.

When living in a hostile environment, the little white boy, Timmy you know he feels comfortable and happy about what his mother has just said about him James looks at his mother and wonders why can't she be proud of him? because he doesn't understand the secret yet and by the time, he learns the secret, he will already have been injured by injured.

REMEMBER, TOO REMEMBER

Annointedhandsfacebook.com

We have no idea how many wives' girlfriends' children inherited the disease and also died or were forever crippled by its effects. For 40 years the U.S. Government operated public health services and conducted what was known as the Tuskegee syphilis study. One of the darkest chapters in American history now over 40 years after the study ended, we still don't know and might never know the full extent of its effects and the study might have continued if not for and 1972 article, and no one said, this is wrong.

Syphilis was considered a National Health crisis, in the early 20th century. Doctors at the time thought syphilis and other medical complications were affected by race, which only affected Africans, that is to say, that Caucasians were pure and lily-white, they couldn't contract such dreadful disease. To study the disease, researchers, found a population of poor black syphilitic sharecroppers, in and around Tuskegee Alabama. During the Great Depression, nearly 400 of the participants had syphilis, while another 200, in the control group, did not. In the end, as many as 100 men died from complications related to untreated syphilis and the message was very clear black deaths mattered.

Medical doctors deliberately let them die and wanted them to die, for what they could discover from their bodies later. The story would be explosive after the story broke and there was this incredible public outcry. Senator Kennedy had held very public congressional hearings on this. If they had been white, your public health service would never have agreed to do the study. the aftermath is well documented in films and books, but there are still things we might never know. We, all know that the answer, it was in the name of modern medicine. But, why this group of people? Because at that time, we were considered less than human.

And years later, we still have not heard the answer to the very simple question of why? Why, the doctors, should have not been able to determine after the first three or four autopsies, that the inside of a black person ravaged by syphilis looks identical to the insides of a white person and stopped the study. There's, no way to know just how many people were directly or adjacently affected by the study. There's still at least one lesson to be learned from the Tuskegee syphilis study, never quit fighting, never quit standing up and yelling from the mountain top, this is wrong.

SHE WAS AND IS IMMORTAL

Black History facebook.com

During the dark days in American medicine, a Black woman does it again. Some, of the most, important advancements in modern medical research, can ultimately be traced back, to the black women and men from our past. Some were farmers and others sharecroppers. But, this heroic woman, who worked on a tobacco farm, before World War Two, her name was Henrietta Lacks.

In February 1951 Henrietta Lacks was diagnosed with an aggressive form of cervical cancer, at the Johns Hopkins Hospital. Not known to her, a sample of her cells, was sent to a tissue lab. A cell biologist, isolated and then multiplied it as it turned out the cells did not die. As would normally be the case and in fact, they were doubling at this phenomenal rate, it would just keep replicating, although these weren't the first human cells grown in a lab, this was the first time they survived more than a few days, outside the human body.

It was a medical breakthrough, the cells were given the name HeLa Cells, a combination of the first two letters of Henrietta lacks first and last name. Although the cells carry her name Lacks, who passed away at the young age of 31, would never know that her cells had been extracted for scientific research. Like so many other contributions, Blacks have made to modern-day scientific discoveries, that were kept hidden from us and the public. Lacks family members, and only learned that her cells had been harvested, 2 decades after her death. a Rolling Stone journalist contacted them and revealed that Lacks cells had been duplicated, and then used for research by countless scientists, the article called the work a critical tool in medical research. Henrietta Lacks cells, have played a crucial role in scientific advancement. The fact, that Lacks herself never consented to the research, means that her cells were used unethically, what's more, her case was part of a long tradition of the use of African American bodies without their consent for medical and scientific research.

Tuskegee syphilis, was part of a culture, of not respecting the core humanity of black folk, and how they were being treated either by medical researchers or even by physicians. Despite, the ethical debate around the harvesting of Lacks cells, scientists have continued to use the immortal HeLa cell line all over the world. Research, involving polio vaccines, chemotherapy, HIV aids cloning and IVF have all benefited from the HeLa cell line.

COME CLEAN OR STAY AWAY DIRTY

Annointed hands Facebook

Why, does racism exist? because the Caucasians we interact with daily, have no intention of letting us know why, or they don't know the reason why either. The people, that classify themselves as Caucasian, love to say that black people are a minority, when in fact we are not a minority. Not only, do white people make up less than 9% of the world population, but they are also, what we call genetically recessive, meaning their genes regardless of who they mix with are masks, or the appearance of who they are isn't shown in the strongest propensity.

You have five groups of people of color the black man, brown man, Redman the yellow man, and the white man, when we come into contact, whether it be a black man or black woman with a white woman or white man although each offspring has a copy of the dominant gene and recessive gene because we as black people are genetically dominant. We, mask the appearance of whiteness, we can look at Barack Obama as having an African father and European mother, but still black, we can look at Anne-Marie has one Asian parent and one black parent however she's still black.

Please always remember, that the very first individual, that was found in this world was a black queen by the nickname, I call Lucy, which was founded in Ethiopia. Showing that, not only is Africa the origins of all humanity and civilization, but it was, a black woman, that was all of us, all of our mitochondrial DNA. The misunderstandings, on who came first were discovered years ago, but why does racism exist. How, we as black people have not been able to love them enough, praise them enough, be tolerant enough, and be diversified and integrated.

Why has no matter what we've done to show this group of people, that we're not Britney not made a difference? It seems that white people, now you're the smallest group of people in the world you're making up less than 9% of the world population, you're dying off sooner than you're being born and then you're genetically recessive, what must you do to ensure that you do not go extinct? To have a better tomorrow is to live a better life today, and love thy neighbor as thy self.

The best opportunity for living or survival, it's always killing the dominant gene, the dominant gene being African people, you must incarcerate the dominant gene because this leads to decreased procreation, the ability of them to share having children. It's about Caucasians, not being genetically annihilated and Africans, not being able to procreate are genetic dominance. Darker, black people are treated the worse because they have more melanin pigment therefore you are more of a threat than many of us cannot truly grasp.

we as Africans, cannot love them out of this, we cannot pray them out of this, it's a matter of life or death for them. I understand that. What is happening to you, you'll understand? OK, this summer will understand oh that's why you keep throwing black men in prison because you don't want them to have children because you don't want us to have because you don't want black men and black women appropriate blackness that we procreate in this world this will go extinct racism exists.

EVERYTHING YOU ARE IS THANKS TO US

Ana Ata Aidoo

The thing is that as far as I'm concerned, since the Africans, met the Europeans over 500 years ago. Look at us, we have given everything, you are still taking, it is true. Where, would the whole western world be without Africa? Our cocoa, our diamonds, our timber, our gold, cobalt and uranium, and other minerals everything you are, is us that is a fact. And in return, for all of this, what have we got? nothing.

antipersonnel indoctrination against ourselves, if you go and cook your horrible diseases, like AIDS, you say it is us. you brought us tuberculosis we didn't have this big cough until white people came to Africa. In exchange, Africa has given us 500 solid years of our people. The western world of our human beings to dig your gold, work in the cane fields, I mean you know fish peanuts, palm224 oil everything in exchange for that, we have gotten nothing and you know nothing, and some white people look upon us as if we were monkeys.

It is true it's in your literature your best thinkers like German people say that we don't even have the brain of animals. The Catholic Church believed, that to enslave an African, is to save his soul, how, from what, the European? You, are where you are, because of Africa. Some ask, don't you think that this type of thinking is over now, is it over, who said that AIDS came from the green monkey, is it over?

FROM THE TRIBE OF JUDAH

Good Vibes Homeopathic Healing

Africans, do you know why the main goal of colonization was to totally depopulate and involuntarily mix the entire African continent to repopulate it with other races? Well, I have a message for African people, if you're not black you can stay, but if you're black, I want you to listen well.

The reason, why history repeats itself, is because the world is a cycle and whatever goes around must come back around. There was a time when Africa ruled Europe for 800 years and when I say rule, not with guns and ammunition, but with knowledge, love, light, and black excellence. So, now I want you to know that we have cycled back to that time. A time, when the kingdom of God, belongs to the poor and the slaves, and mine is just to curtain raise. Yours is to step into your awareness of self, yours is to go back within and get into union with your ancestors.

your DNA, get your ancestral membership back, and remember all that you are, because among you at the descendants of the likes, Mansa Musa kings and queens, among you are the DNA of the TALAI the tribe of the lion of Judah, are the inventors of the hieroglyphics, among you are the architectures of the great pyramids, the incredible mathematics of the ISHANGO BONE, among you, are the DNA of the Moors, the teachers, of all modern European technology.

Among you, are the DNA that mentored great European philosophers like Pythagoras, who studied in Africa for 22 years. As a black person, the DNA of slavery and colonization is not the only DNA that you carry, and they know that. The ancient great African civilization is still present imprinted deep in your soul. They can ban all the books; ancient African books were stolen and some burnt to hide knowledge of self. All Ancient African Universities were left in ruins, but your DNA is present, your memory is present, and your ancestral knowledge is present deep in your soul and is yours forever.

There was a time, they wanted to wipe us all off or mix us all up, so there was no one left to remember. There, was a time that remembering who you are would have been a great crime and so the ancestors had you forget to protect yourself. But I am here to assure you, that it is safe to remember, the African royalties among you. It is time for black people to experience the excellence of their blackness, it is time to awaken the extreme talents and excellence that are deeply rooted within you it is now safe to show the world and join into one with your ancestors.

P.S.

Jane Elliot

Take a lesson from history. Some people asked, why didn't President O' Bama do more for Blacks? He is still alive, Martin L. King is dead, and Malcolm X is dead because they spoke out against the tyranny of blacks in America would surely mean death for him.

They were all killed, not because of the color of their skin, but because Caucasians feared, that someone who is not a Caucasian is going to look better, sound better, and do better than they are doing. So, when someone says "Make America Great Again" what they really mean is making America hate again.

America, prepared for WW II in six months. Racism is a created evil, anything that is created can be dissolved. Caucasians, created racism, God created the human race and it started with a black woman. If I could stand before the Caucasian race and speak, I would say, first understand yourself?

You have been and still, are the destroyer of nations, civilizations, and dreams, then you call us savages. If anyone wants to be treated well in the future, you have to treat others well in the present.

WHO WILL CRY FOR MOTHER AFRICA?

David Haywood

Who will cry for mother Africa?

Left to fend for herself.

Who will cry for mother Africa?

She educated the western world seven times.

Who will cry for mother Africa?

She cried and cried but there is no sleep or rest for her.

Who will cry for mother Africa?

Whose people were taken to faraway places and shores?

Who will cry for mother Africa?

Who was raped time and time again?

Who will cry for mother Africa?

Who knew well, hurt and pain.

Who will cry for mother Africa?

She gave from her heart and soul without regret, who will come to her aid?

14 BLACK INVENTORS

African Diaspora facebook.com

who the world owes gratitude for their inventions the contributions of black inventors to the technological advancement of the world are one subject that must always be in the spotlight of black history all year round, and not just a topic to be discussed during Black History Month? in a world where African American history has become a threat to so many circles, a true and holistic account of the black inventors in American history is important to further point to the ingenuity of black people worldwide.

let's brag a little about the inventions of African Americans and how black people are not worthless like European scholars and white supremacists will have you believe from the traffic light to elevators and images of space, black inventors in history have revolutionized the way we live and understand the universe. most people are familiar with well-known inventions such as the lightbulb cotton gin and iPhone but there are innumerable additional things that make our life easier that are often forgotten.

African American inventors are among the creative innovators behind these devices in this article we furnish you with a list of black inventors and the inventions that have come from their thoughts ranging from traffic lights to security systems, blood banks, lightbulb filaments, and so on. Jesse Eugene Russell invented the digital cell phone in 1988.

In 1988 while working as an engineer at AT&T Bell laboratories Jesse Eugene Russell- invented the wireless digital phone and communication system, he invented the world's first digital cellular base station and has the patent for many of the digital services that are used today.

Dr. Gladys West- invented the Global Positioning System (GPS) she was the brains behind the design and calibration of the GPS, which the entire world now uses.

Sarah Marshall Boone- invented the improved ironing board in 1892.

Mary Van Brittan Brown- invented the home security system in 1966.

Garrett Morgan- invented the Traffic Signal and Gas Mask in 1923.

Frederick Mc Kinley Jones- invented refrigerated trucks in 1940, now day Thermo-King.

Alexander Miles- Automatic Elevator doors in 1887.

James E. West- Co-invented the Electret Microphone in 1964, which is now used in hearing aids.

Lewis Latimer- invented the carbon light bulb filament in 1881.

Mark Dean Co- invented the color IBM PC monitor and the Gigahertz chip between 1980 and 1999.

Madam CJ Walker- invented specialized hair care products in 1905.

George Washington Carver- The most prominent Black Scientist of the 20th century.

Valerie Thomas- invented the illusion transmitter for outer space in 1976.

Dr. Charles Drew- invented the blood bank in1941.

THE WAR ON AFRICAN MALES

Cocoa Butter facebook.com

You have the right to remain silent, anything you do or say will not matter at this point because your skin color is already confessed to the crime. You have the right to an attorney, who will try his hardest to see that justice is served in a jury of our peers, aka OUR attorneys, who will have our backs 12 to one. If you cannot afford an attorney, one will be appointed to you free of charge, because he's also on our payroll.

Do you understand these rights as they have been read to you? Woah, Woah, I see you reaching for your nine-millimeter wallet. I see you reaching for your 38-caliber inhaler, don't move to stop breathing, you're puffing up your chest! I feel threatened! Is that a weapon? laid down low, face down, no! Face ground. Pow! Oops, I did it again.

I'm a pop star. No, I'm a cop star. By the time I get back to the precinct, I'll be a rock star. Clap for 'em. I have more black names on trophies than BET Award winners.

Clap for 'em. They are going to honor me at the NYPD Award Dinner. Clap for 'em. They are going to throw me a parade. Clap for 'em. Because when I clap for them, they go to the grave. Black boys' tears fall on deaf white ears.

Black mothers' tears keep graveyard grass green. Black men's bones are the gravel that finalizes false convictions. on the Galaxy which finalized false convictions. Wake up, black boys. It's time to declare war. I wonder how Trayvon Martin's mother feels that her son has a household name, but not a household body. I wonder if Freddie Gray's family can still say grace over their food even though their prayers cannot stop the thief that robbed him of his last breath. I wonder if Tamir Rice died playing cops and robbers because he saw the former as more innocent than the latter. I wonder if black mothers are only closer to God because they're steady having to lay rest to their only begotten sons.

I wonder, if black people are only darker because we are closer to the sun, well how many years will it take for us to become bulletproof because we're closer to the gun?

I'm tired of going to funerals where babies are buried in bigger boxes than they used to put their toys in. I'm tired of not being able to tell my friends to see you later. We steadily practiced our goodbye words to each other. I'm tired because I'm not able to tell my girlfriend, let's wait 'til we're married.

I'm afraid she'll see me in a box before she sees me in a tuxedo. I wonder if America when she wakes up and sees that black people aren't sleeping anymore because the American dream is the African American nightmare. I'm tired that laws are written as lullabies to black people, and I'm forced to stay woke in this society. black people and if I go back to sleep, I might stay asleep

www.ingramcontent.com/pod-product-compliance
Lightning Source LLC
Chambersburg PA
CBHW031255160726
47993CB00001B/175